Soul of a Second Skin
The Journey of a Gay Christian Leatherman

First Edition

Published by The Nazca Plains Corporation
Las Vegas, Nevada
2007

ISBN: 978-1-934625-38-5

Published by

The Nazca Plains Corporation®
4640 Paradise Rd, Suite 141
Las Vegas NV 89109-8000

© 2007 by The Nazca Plains Corporation. All rights reserved.

No part of this work may be reproduced or utilized in any form or by any means, electronic or mechanical, including photocopying, microfilm, and recording, or by any information storage and retrieval system, without permission in writing from the publisher. Printed in the United States of America.

Cover, Hardy Haberman
Art Director, Blake Stephens

Dedication

I have been very lucky in my life. I have had a loving and understanding family who supports not only my being gay, but my leather/BDSM/fetish life as well. I have a host of friends whose constant encouragement and advice enriches my life. I have a miraculous church family that celebrates my sexuality with me. I have a loving partner who makes my life richer than he could ever know. It is to these people and the numerous family and leatherfolk who go before me that I dedicate this book.

I also want to dedicate it to my friends Roger Stabel and his late partner Jackson Myars without whom I might never have found my path to Christianity.

"God loved the world so much, that Jesus Christ, God's only begotten Son, was freely given, that whosoever believes in Him shall not perish but have everlasting life." John 3:16

Soul of a Second Skin
The Journey of a Gay Christian Leatherman

First Edition

Hardy Haberman

Contents

Introduction

As I sit down to write this book I am amazed at my own hubris. How could I ever hope to put on paper any kind of theological musings, especially the kind that would relate to the kind of radical sexuality with which I identify? My religious training consists mainly of what I learned in religious school as a Reform Jew and the few courses I took attending a Southern Baptist University. What big balls I must have to try to write about spirituality when I have no PhD after my name or a university position in my resume?

As I asked myself these questions and a couple of hundred more, I found the answer. There is one subject I am the undisputed expert on and that is me. I am the only person who has had my particular faith journey. I am the only person to know what is going on in my spirituality. I am the only person who knows my story, and when I look at it that way, I have the fortitude to write.

This book really evolved from an article I wrote several years ago for the online magazine, whosoever.com. In that piece, I began this task, and now several years later it has finally made it to print.

When I first became involved in the Leather/BDSM/Fetish scene, there were no books about leather spirituality. There were no articles about the "Zen of Bondage" or the "Slave Spirit". My friends and I just groped in the darkness and with each other's help we found our way. There were a few books like Larry Townsend's *Leatherman's Handbook* and later Geoff Means' *Urban Aboriginal* but beyond that material related to spirituality was minimal. People talked about it, but only a few had any grasp of what was going on.

Today, there are lots of articles about it, and to avoid cluttering up that niche, I will try to keep from making broad pronouncements. I will try to keep the New Age metaphors to a minimum and leave chakras, auras and other manifestations to another writer.

What I am going to write about is personal and in many ways conventional. However, it is my hope that this story will reveal something non-conventional; a new way of looking at some established theological concepts and a fresh view of what it means to be spiritual and religious. For those unfamiliar with the leather community and BDSM in general I have included an appendix with a workable introduction to the lifestyle. I encourage you to keep an open mind both in regard to BDSM and my discussions of spirituality.

Now in regard to sexuality, I will speak frankly and not pull punches. I think to try to soft pedal the sexual aspects of this topic would be doing a disservice to my reader and to the importance of the sexual component. For those who might be a bit squeamish about reading or talking about sex, I suggest that you be brave and keep reading. Though you might be shocked, or maybe in some cases a little titillated, just be assured that sex is something that is common to all human experience.

I often wonder if people really consider the profound implications of Jesus as being a real human being. Whether you believe he was God incarnate, the Son of God or just a man, the human condition includes sex as part of it. Does that mean Jesus had sex? I don't know, but I do know that sexuality is integral to what it means to be human, so I guess the jury will be out on that for a while.

I will try to keep references to a minimum, but I will include a bibliography at the end of this book for those of you who might be interested in the material I have read on my faith journey. I will also quote occasionally from scriptures, and for that I use both the King James Version and the New Revised Standard Version of the Bible.

It is my hope that in some way this story will inspire other kinky folk to explore their own spiritual experiences and to find a path that allows for both radical sexuality and religion. That's what this books is really about, finding the path that worked for me. It will not work for everyone, but it might give a few hints as to the direction to travel.

May your journey be fulfilling and leave a trail of people who are better for having known you.

Hardy Haberman

Meeting God in a Dungeon

Until I became part of Inquisition Dallas, I had never played in a "commercial dungeon". For those who don't know, and I am sure that is most of you, Inquisition Dallas was a warehouse that me and five of my friends rented and turned into a play space. We had no illusions of making any money with it. What we did want was to have a place where Leathermen and Leatherwomen in Dallas and North Texas could come and find that elusive domain known as "Leatherspace".

We painted the walls with a grey stone pattern as our concession to theatrics, and set about putting together equipment and areas ideal for SM activities. If you haven't figured out by now, I like BDSM, more specifically the SM part. Sadomasochism has a really bad name. What we do in a play space or dungeon has little to do with the Marquis de Sade whose name forms a part of the acronym. We practice a safe, sane and consensual offshoot which has more to do with a mutually satisfying and exciting experience than the libertine abuses our friend the Marquis was fond of.

We added a small room at the entrance of the building for socializing and snacks. This social area was meant as a place where people could relax and "come down" from a scene and a place to talk and negotiate for play.

We made it comfortable and well lit and with the exception of a few black and white photos, it gave no clue of the activities that took place beyond the black door to the dungeon.

A couch and a couple of chairs were it as far as furnishings, along with a long table that could be set with food and snacks for the events. It was also the only carpeted part of the building, since we needed a floor that was easily cleaned, the rest remained concrete.

Aside from the restrooms and a soft drink machine, that was it for creature comforts. As Spartan as it was, it seemed elaborate compared to the places we had played in the past. My crowd played in peoples garages, basements, abandoned warehouses and sometimes outside at a remote kink friendly campground. We didn't have the luxury of a clubhouse like some large cities, and backrooms at the bars had gone the way of the dodo bird.

The majority of the place was given over to Leatherspace and when it was populated by BDSM enthusiasts the whole character of the place changed. We had over a dozen stations designed for our play. There were St. Andrew's Crosses, slings, hanging cages, tables, pillories and simple attachment points along the walls with chains hanging, ready for action. Each station was lit with a spotlight, or more accurately a clamp-light with a relatively dim colored bulb. These lights were the only illumination, and they clearly lit and defined the areas for play. The floor was marked off with yellow caution-tape to mark limits around each station and give observers a guideline as to how close they could stand to watch. This was our concession to the voyeurs, since not everyone at a play party will be playing at all times, and some of them are relative newcomers, the tape helped remind people to stay back a respectful and safe distance from the players.

Safety was a big part of the design. For SM scenes involving whips or floggers, we included sufficient space to assure that bystanders would not be accidentally caught in a backswing. We also provided all our equipment with "panic snaps". These were quick disconnect attachment points so people in bondage could be extricated quickly and safely if needed. Fire exits and extinguishers were well marked and checked regularly, and we even had special work lights that could be turned on to provide bright illumination if needed for cleaning or for emergencies.

We also installed a music system scrounged from donated components. The music we played made a big difference on the way a party went. We spend a lot of time collecting music that would help set the mood for a gathering. My friends and I had similar tastes and the playlist often included trance, new-age electronic, ethereal techno-dance and sometimes world beat selections. The key to any music we played was that it could accompany and drive a scene, not overwhelm it. CW and rock and roll were off the menu, usually. We even built a basic DJ booth so we could have a live DJ mixing music for special occasions. When that did occur the effect was absolutely magical. Just as a knowledgeable DJ can keep a dance floor active, a kink-aware DJ can keep a dungeon party really energetic!

The lighting, music and general ambience of the place gave it an unmistakable feel. It was sexy. It felt slightly grungy and somewhat illicit. The moody lighting gave plenty of visibility to play, but focused attention not on the décor but the play. There was a Spartan eroticism to the place that spoke of power, submission and a lot of raw masculinity. That last element was not intended as a sexual slight to women, just a nod to the aggressive energy that the space exuded. Over the years it existed we got a myriad of compliments from some of the most notable folks in the leather/BDSM/fetish scene about the amazing spirit of our dungeon. I still have people comment to me on how special Inquisition was. But it wasn't just the surroundings that made it special.

As my friends and I formed a club of SM players to inhabit the place, we were careful to screen out the sexual tourists and gawkers that such activity attracts. Oh there would be no problem with a member watching a scene, but the real attraction was a place to play, unimpeded by the inherent problems of non-dedicated facilities. Since we were in a warehouse district, there was a lot of parking and very few neighbors at night. The noises and activity of our parties would be almost invisible to the other tenants of the area who were long gone before our gatherings started.

The group of people who made up our membership became a family. There were old guard leathermen, hard core leatherdykes, kinky straight couples, enthusiastic novices and seasoned players. The real requirement for membership was a desire to participate and an understanding of what we were trying to create. All our members helped mold the warehouse into real Leatherspace.

During a party you might see a group of people in wearing their fetishes gathered in the social room. There would be the same chat and camaraderie as any party of friends, but beyond the dungeon door, things changed. Conversations ceased and the spirit of leather took over. The music, the lighting the sights and the smells drove your senses into a state that was at its heart erotic. There was a reverence for the space that defied a visitor to break the atmosphere. When you went into the dungeon, you knew there was something special going on.

For people playing in the dungeon our scenes seemed more intense. It wasn't that we were playing any more vigorously than we might somewhere else, but the space seemed so focused it seemed to amplify every aspect of the play. People rarely had conversations in the dungeon; instead they participated or watched in reverence to something almost sacred.

It seems a little odd to speak of a dungeon full of Leather/BDSM/Fetish enthusiasts as a sacred space, but in one sense it was. The play that went on there was a form of very physical communion between the players. Though sexual intercourse was rarely part of the activity, since our house rules didn't allow it at a public party, there was a level of intimacy that was certainly profound and erotic. It carried with it the same kind of intimacy that you might find in a church or other sacred space.

Now I am not trying to say our dungeon was a church or anything remotely like a church, but the experience of Leatherspace carried with it a reverence. Just as in a church, the only noises that seem appropriate are sacred music and prayer, in our dungeon the only sounds appropriate were a special kind of music and the sounds of BDSM play.

It is no accident we named our group Inquisition. We discussed many names but that one stuck and I believe it is because of its religious history. Perhaps the darkest period of the church was during the Inquisition, torture and death of innocent people was commonplace. The Inquisition, particularly the Spanish Inquisition was often brutal and sadistic. Since many times cruelty is associated in the public mind with our activities, we felt using the name Inquisition might make us seem a little more serious than other groups. Additionally, we felt that by taking that name we could transform it into something vastly different than its namesake.

As leatherfolk, we are people of transcendence. We engage in activities most people would find unpleasant and yet we find in them the seeds of something erotic. We take implements of torture like whips and floggers, tools for punishment and pain in the hands of most people. In the hands of a leatherman or woman those weapons are transformed into sex toys for our pleasure. We take bondage and restriction conditions that most people would find intolerable and yet in those we find a freedom and release unmatched anywhere. It is that same thinking that guided us to take the name of the Inquisition. In history the Inquisition was a name to be feared. Under our control, the Inquisition became a symbol of positive energy, intimacy and camaraderie.

It is in that special place where Leatherspace could exist that I took what was just one more step in my journey of spirituality. I sincerely believe that sometimes the scenes taking place in the dungeon moved beyond simple BDSM play. I had several experiences where I felt I was in touch not just with my play partner but with something greater than either of us.

Sometimes when leatherfolk play, especially in a very intense scene, they reach a place where both players strip away the veneer of civilization and touch something primal. The sounds that emanate from a bottom or submissive as they pass through the haze of pain and move into the grey area between pain and pleasure are astounding. They are from deep in the soul, a long repressed place where the line between humanity and beast blurs.

It is at that moment when something amazing occurs. The energies being released become palpable. The Top or Dominant moves beyond just the person delivering a sensation, be it from a whip, a flogger, a hand or any other tool, into an active participant in the experience of the sub or bottom. He or she becomes both the instigator of the sensation and the vicarious recipient in the form of the reactions from the bottom or sub. The interplay of body language and vocalization draw both people into communion. It is a sacred sharing of the experience, and I believe it is something even greater.

I use the word communion for a purpose. Much like the Christian church, I believe when leatherfolk are in communion with each other they are also in communion with all those who have gone before us. Much like the Communion of the Saints, I think we find our deepest connections with our leather spirit and our leather brothers and sisters in our play.

It is no accident that Jesus used a physical act, the sharing of a common meal, as the key to a connection to all his followers. Repeating that act joins Christians not only with Christ and the Holy Spirit but with the generations of disciples who performed the same act. In some way, the communion in the dungeon acts in a similar fashion.

Before I am accused of heresy, let me assure you that I am not equating the sharing of communion, a key sacrament in my church, to a scene in the dungeon. However, I use the example to give some insight into the profound connection BDSM play can have. I also feel that anytime we make deep connections like those in our play, we in some way connect with the divine.

That connection has been vital in my spiritual journey. I feel it not only in the dungeon, but at home when I am in the company of my partner, Patrick. My boy (that is what I call him, though he is very much an adult) and I share a deep love and commitment that transcends friendship. We communicate both verbally and physically in our play and lovemaking in a way that I feel makes that same kind of connection with the divine.

What I am talking about is love. Though it may seem odd, I feel I cannot play with a partner without having a love for him or her that is deep enough to be worthy of the trust needed to play together. It is not the same love I have for my boy, or the same love I have for God, but it is love all the same. Though it seems strange to an outsider to speak of BDSM as love, I can assure you that for me, it is. The physical acts in the dungeon would be simple assault without the key element of love. The mutual respect and trust of the players, is one manifestation of this. The care a Top or Dominant takes to bring a bottom or sub to that peak experience of a scene is an act of love. The offering of his or her body for the pleasure and use by the Top is an act of love.

How odd it must seem to someone who has never experienced it? That two people involved in a flogging or bondage could be doing something sacred. That truth will probably remain accessible only to those who have had the experience. To someone who does not understand the dynamics of the power exchange in the dungeon, it will always be somewhat a mystery. But to those who have experienced it, even if you are only a novice, I would ask you to think about this communion the next time you play. Don't clutter your mind with preconceived goals in mind, but simply be with your partner in that intimate place only Leatherspace can provide. Let the dance of sensations, emotions and communication wrap you in its embrace and find the sharing of something beyond yourself. To me, that is the key.

I also urge you to find a way to make your play space something special as well. Be it a warehouse, a bedroom or a remote outdoor spot, treat it as Leatherspace. Giving a part of your environment over to Leatherspace is a sacrifice as well. It means reserving that place for the special activities we leatherfolk share. Perhaps that sacrifice can serve to make not only that space but the activities as well, special, and in doing so, will honor the acts that take place there. Make it something sacred and special where you and your partners can be open to that unique communion BDSM play can become.

Finding a God Who Knows I'm Kinky

As a child, I spent a lot of Sundays in religious school. That is what we called the place we went to learn about Reform Judaism. Since Saturday was the Sabbath, and no one was supposed to work, the school met on Sunday, much like Christian Sunday Schools. That is where the similarity stopped. We studied the history of the Jewish people both from a pure historical standpoint and a Biblical perspective. It gave me a good indoctrination into what gentiles call the Old Testament and we called the Torah and the Holy Scriptures.

Additionally, I took Hebrew lessons. I learned how to decipher the strange backward reading alphabet of a language that was spoken only in the Jewish church and the far off land of Israel. It was all in preparation for the day when at 13 years of age I would have my Bar Mitzvah. That is the coming-of-age ceremony Jewish boys go through to formally become part of the congregation. It meant I would have to read the Torah in Hebrew in front of a packed Temple full of my friends and relatives. It was nerve wracking!

I was no stranger to performing, since from the age of ten I had been an amateur magician, but this was different. At the time I was still an undiagnosed dyslexic, and the strings of Hebrew characters gave me fits when trying to decipher them. Additionally, as a magician, I was used to thinking on my feet. I could improvise and basically BS my way through almost anything. As the Bar Mitzvah boy, I was expected to give an eloquent reading of the selected passage on the Torah and a short prepared speech.

It may have been at that point that I understood the meaning of the word "humiliation". What on earth were these people thinking? I could probably bluff my way through the event, except that there would be people, old people, in the front row who could actually speak Hebrew! They would know if I was faking it or not and I was not just reading he phone book, I was reading the words of Moses! My accent was great, and I hoped that would count for something, but alas it did not.

When the big day came, I stood before the congregation in my yarmulke and tallis (prayer shawl) and stuttered and stumbled on every word. I sweat like the proverbial whore in church. I felt naked, alone, embarrassed and slightly aroused. Oops!

Something had gone wrong with my bodies wiring. I should have been losing control of my bladder and instead my putz was growing inside my new pair of black wool slacks. Thank God there was a sturdy lectern blocking anyone from seeing. I only hoped God would forgive my hard-on that pressed against it.

When I finished the reading and my remarks, I tugged my prayer shawl down on one side a little so it covered the bulge in my pants and I sat back down. Later everyone complimented me on my work, though I knew it sucked, and presented me with a shower of gifts, including at least 10 fountain pens.

I learned a lot that day. First I learned, thankfully, that none of my relatives except my Grandmother and Uncle Harry read Hebrew. Next, I learned that the stress of humiliation could have a very unexpected effect on a man's body. That last bit I tucked away for later use.

More importantly, I learned that God wasn't going to strike me dead for screwing up the reading from the sacred scrolls. God was not going to strike me down for being nervous, and lastly that God didn't care if I had an erection in the Temple or not. To this day no one else ever knew, and with that big a secret, you'd figure if God was the psychopathic smite-and-plague kind of God I read about in the Old Testament. Then either he wasn't all-knowing, or he really had no problem with a teenagers oddball sexual quirks. Eventually, I settled on the latter, but not before doing a lot of looking and experimenting.

Following my Bar Mitzvah I attended services on Friday night with my parents and really began enjoying the church. We had a rabbi who was a firebrand in not only Texas but the whole country. Rabbi Levi Olan was an activist. He marched with civil rights workers across the South and that made the congregation nervous. He spoke about social justice and reconciliation and that got a few folks upset. He even came out against the Vietnam War, and with that the congregation really began to squirm in their seats.

I loved hearing him! He was always challenging our intellects and beliefs and always managed to find the justification for it in scripture. What I learned in those pews was that people throughout history had profound experiences with the divine. They heard God speaking and many, like the prophets, used those words to speak truth to the power of the day. That underlying truth has stayed with me always. I discovered a God who seemed to favor people who made the status quo uncomfortable. God favored people who sought justice and equality. Outcasts, the oddballs and the out-of-the-mainstream are often the heroes in many biblical stories.

Abraham and his wife Sarah were geezers. They were an old childless couple who at the time were marginalized and even shamed. Surprise! God chose Sarah to mother the lineage that would become the people of Israel.

David was a scrawny kid who tagged along with the army. Too young and skinny to put up a fight. Surprise! God chose David to be the one to defeat Goliath the Philistine, and do it with not armor and a sword, but a sling and a rock. Talk about odd.

The list is long and strange from Noah, a crazy man who built a boat in the desert to Moses the discarded child who became leader of the Jews. In fact, this was driven home to me every year during the Passover meal. Jews celebrate Passover in their homes with a feast and ceremonies every night for 8 days. One of the readings that is repeated during that service emphasizes the importance of being different. Psalm 118:22, "The stone which the builders rejected has become the chief corner stone."

Still as a teenager, I didn't fully comprehend the meaning of all this and by the time I was about to enter college I had more questions than answers about God. In the fall of my final year of High School my mother showed up at the door to my classroom and called me outside. What she told me rocked the foundations of my world.

My father had died of a heart attack that morning. I was crushed. From the day of his funeral on, I stopped attending the Temple and began questioning the whole God thing. Looking back, I am not surprised. I don't think I was very mature for a 17 year old, and I suspect that since I was already having problems with my sexual yearnings, the death of my father pushed me past the tipping point as far as God was concerned.

The following year I was off to college and since my father was dead, and my grade point average stunk, (as I said I was an undiagnosed dyslexic at the time) I had few choices of schools. My dad had taught at the Baylor Dental School in Dallas and this gave me an automatic entry into Baylor University in Waco. The reduced tuition and the close proximity to Dallas really helped, too. Our family had never been rich and even though there was an insurance settlement when my father died, it left us far from economically secure.

So, off went the now secular Jewish kid to what was then a Southern Baptist university. Talk about culture shock. I had a lot of life changing events happen that year, but few had the impact of attending Baylor. The first year at college is hard anyway, but Baylor in the 60's was a real shock. It was one of the only schools to still have the barbaric practice of freshman hazing. New students were forced to wear green and gold beanies and had to go through lots of humiliation in our daily routines, including opening doors and doing menial tasks for upperclassmen. And I wasn't even pledging a fraternity!

To add to my mortification, word soon got out that I was Jewish and before long I became the class project for divinity students. As the only Jew at Baylor, "witnessing" me became a cottage industry. Hardly a day went by that I wasn't invited to find Jesus Christ as my own personal Lord and savior.

Even more disturbing was my discovery that I really liked guys a lot better than girls. I dated a few girls in college, but I had a lot more fun hanging out with the ROTC guys and watching them polish boots. Also I enjoyed having sex with guys a whole lot more than with girls.

Luckily, by the end of the school year my councilor told me I might be happier at a different school. I never thanked him for that suggestion, but it was exactly the advice I needed. I spent only one year at Baylor and am grateful I never returned. I suspect I would have never become a Christian if I had been exposed to that brand of the religion for another 3 years.

As I matured both sexually and spiritually I experimented with everything from Wicca to Transcendental Meditation and never found a place where I felt truly at home. Now I know my problem was I was looking for a religious tradition that included me rather than excluded me. Not only did I know I was gay, but I knew I had yearnings for something more, something my friends told me was dark and dangerous.

Eventually, years later I found my way into a Unitarian Universalist church and ended up smiling all the way through the service. The congregation was open and accepting and very liberal. I could bring the best of my Jewish traditions with me and find a community of people who were actively seeking to grow spiritually. It was a good place for me to begin developing an image of a God who could accept me for all the different things I was.

I had come-out into leather a few years earlier, and my leather life was under development as well. I had met a man who seemed to enjoy some of the same kinky things I did and he soon become my lover and my boy. He was spontaneous, charming and had a great sense of humor, all of which were important to me. Unfortunately, leather for him was a passing fad. He thought of it as mere theatrics and though we remained partners, the Daddy/boy part of the relationship faded and eventually disappeared.

At that time I too drifted away from leather and lost touch with my leather mentors and buddies. We moved to a comfy suburban home and started living a largely vanilla life. With the exception of our wild parties, we were pretty average suburban gays. It was the wild parties that became the problem.

Several years into the relationship I began to suspect that something was really wrong. Normal folks didn't go through a trunk-load of liquor at every party. Normal folks, even those who were gay, didn't spend a lot of their time cleaning up from the blackouts of their partners. Normal folks didn't run around town paying off their partner's drug dealers. Normal folks didn't find themselves at Tax time facing a stack of ATM receipts for $100 a pop that totaled to around $35,000 for the year!

My partner realized the problem before me and trotted himself to Alcoholics Anonymous just in time. Only a few months later would I end up in the Al-Anon room taking care of my own addiction. That was a good thing, too.

The 12 step program of Al-Anon/AA got me back in touch with my "higher power". Eventually that would become God, and a God who could accept all of me, faults, addictions, sexual preferences and kink. Working the 12 steps gave me a chance to assess who I was and what I was doing. It was a lot of hard work, and occasionally still is, but I kept with the program and eventually the Cocaine Anonymous program where I face my drug problem.

All this time I was attending the Unitarian Church with my partner, but that was about to change. Eventually he decided that being in a relationship with me was not what he wanted and we separated amicably. I got the house and the dogs. He got the church.

What I was left with was a yearning for that shared experience of worship that a church brings. I yearned for a contact with God and it would be a few years until I settled in a church home where I could not only be who I was, but wear my leathers to the service! Still I had the beginnings of a spirituality that has stayed with me and a God who not only knew I was gay and kinky, but celebrated that kink with me.

Finding My Leather Soul

Sometime in 1976, just before the Village People really made their splash, I found myself gravitating toward guys in leather. The motorcycle jackets, caps, chaps and boots held a fascination for me and they still do. I had started to become politically active since the gay and lesbian community in Dallas was starting to flex its collective muscles.

I had come out in the gay sense at the end of the 1960's and remember scampering out of a nightclub as the police raided the place for a variety of infractions including male/male dancing and female impersonation. Back then gays were regularly beat up in local parks and gay men were rounded up in police sweeps of nightclubs that catered to the gay crowd.

By the 1970's the movement started at Stonewall was reaching Dallas and I took a stand, marching in one of the early gay protests which eventually become Gay Pride parades. The Texas Sodomy Law was used as justification for not only harassment but discrimination in every aspect of a person's life. The law known as 2106, the number of the statute in the state penal code really dominated gay politics. I joined the Dallas Gay Political Caucus and become active in the movement to try to get the law overturned. It was there that I first got to know a few leathermen. Leather activists were non-existent at that time. We were all just gays trying to fight for the right to be left alone. In there were lots of women involved in the movement as well, but at the time many of them considered themselves "gay" as well. It was a big, all-encompassing term.

Though I was attracted to guys in leather, I really didn't know what leather was all about. I just knew there was something there I really wanted. I hadn't figured out the details, but I knew seeing guys in leather jackets and pants and chaps dominated my fantasies. It became so powerful that it finally moved me into action.

Off the beaten path and many blocks away from the "gay-berhood" of the Oak Lawn area of Dallas was a small street in the Little Mexico section of town. It was definitely the wrong side of the tracks for most gay men. Yet, there on that street were two bars that definitely didn't cater to the Mexican-American residents of the area.

One large flat warehouse building was a place called Tex's Ranch. It was a cowboy bar, and had all the appearances of being a mainstream Texas honky-tonk. There was even a western wear store attached to it. Across the parking lot was a low cinderblock building painted completely black. This was the Sundance Kids, a genuine honest-to-God leather bar. Outside on any night were an assortment of motorcycles and trucks, and watching people go in and out it was evident who the patrons were.

I sat in that parking lot many nights watching guys go in. I watched from my van, knowing I needed to get out and go in there, but I was scared shitless. The men who went in and out, at least during the winter months wore lots of leather. They had on vests that displayed the logos of various motorcycle clubs and other organizations. More importantly they looked hot! I was scared, but I sat there with a raging erection, that was how powerful my attraction was.

Not having a motorcycle, I felt out of place. The early 70's were a time when most leathermen in Dallas were bikers and I had no idea if they would accept someone who didn't ride. At least that was the excuse I told myself to keep me safe in my vehicle and out of the bar.

Finally, the urge was too much and I left the safety of my Chevy van and walked toward the door. A couple of guys were hanging out outside and they smiled momentarily at me, the bearded guy in the new leather jacket heading into the bar. Inside, once my eyes got used to the dim lighting I found a scene not much different than any other bar, with the exception of the sheer volume of guys in leather!

I wandered around a little before finding a spot near the cash register at the bar. The bartender, a tall muscled guy with long blond hair turned to me and asked for my order. As I asked for a Martini, straight up, he smiled and reached for a bottle of beer.

"So you wanted a beer, huh?"

I took the bottle and looked at him with a puzzled look.

"You are new here, aren't you?"

I took a sip of beer and nodded.

"I get the feeling you want to fit in," he said, "and carrying around a martini might send the wrong signals."

"Thanks," I said sheepishly.

"Relax," he said with a comforting tone in his voice, "we don't bite unless you ask us to real nice."

And so I took my beer and moved to a nearby wall. Leaning there I watched the bar and got a better feel for the subtle dance that was taking place. I had cruised plenty, but that had been in a disco where the music and lights shielded you from any real interaction other than a glance or a nod. Here, though there was music, the main attraction was not a dance floor, it was the men.

I learned the ins and outs of leather cruising in that bar and with them I began to understand the leather protocol. If you wore your keys on the left, you were a Top and if you wore them on the right you were a bottom. That was the same in the discos, but here there were other silent signals. Hankies, insignia, armbands, collars and caps all were part of the leather vocabulary, and sometimes you had to be extra observant to know what was being said.

Both Tops and bottoms, Daddies and boys wore the traditional motorcycle caps that have become icons of the leather scene. Top's hats had a chrome strip on the brim and bottoms didn't. Occasionally, someone wore a ball cap or even cowboy hat making the signals a little harder to read. Boots were ubiquitous, both cowboy and military. Occasionally, someone would walk through wearing honest-to-god police motorcycle boots. I wore black harness boots, but I aspired to a shiny pair of knee high motorcycle boots. Something in me really like the idea of those!

During my first few forays to the leather bar I stood and watched. Since I wore my keys on the left and usually wore mirrored sunglasses, few people approached me. That was just fine by me. I was nervous and had no idea of what to do if I was actually engaged in conversation. I figured whoever spoke to me would figure out pretty quickly that I didn't belong or at the very least was clueless. I opted for being the strong silent type, waiting for the right moment or for the right moment to come to me.

The Sundance Kids had a small leather shop on its lower level. Near the pool tables a row of counters stretched along one wall. There in a small alcove a large man with a shaved head spent most of the evening pounding rivets into leather straps or helping customers with harnesses, poppers or other goodies.

I gravitated toward that part of the bar, partly for someplace to be, and partly because all the leather clothing and accessories drew me in. I managed to strike up a conversation with the clerk and after a few weeks, we became friends. He could tell I was new and green, and he helped clue me into the protocol and the whole scene.

Once I had become more comfortable, I even managed to strike up conversations with other Tops and even was approached by a few bottoms and boys. It was around that time that I saw a familiar face. My friend Gary from the Gay Political Caucus was among the crowd. I caught his eye and we struck up a conversation. He had seen me in a leather jacket before but didn't know if I was in the leather scene or not. I confessed to him my novice status and he chuckled.

"Everyone is a novice at some point." Gary said.

That went a long way toward making me feel more at home. We discussed our mutual attractions for leather and he gave me a little insight into what it was that leathermen actually did. It was during those first discussions that I first learned about SM. Before long I felt comfortable enough to actually commit to a grey hanky for my left pocket. That meant I was a Top, looking for someone into bondage and light SM as a submissive or bottom. I knew I was turned on by the idea of tying guys up ever since I was a child. I played Cowboys and Indians simply so I could tie the other kids to a tree!

It's funny how childhood experiences often foreshadow what you end up doing in your later life. I have often mused that being kinky may be as much genetics as anything. I have spoken with numerous leatherfolk who told me similar experiences. Seems a lot of us liked tying our friends up.

At Sundance Kids, I also took another step. I bought my first harness from the leather shop. The friendly clerk not only helped me pick it out, but helped me put it on in the dressing area. That was a revelation. It was a complex harness with lots of chrome studs and leather straps, and a couple of straps down the back and front that connected to a ring at my crotch. He showed me how to get my cock and balls through it resulting in an immediate and painful erection.

It felt great! Though it wasn't the kind of harness we now know as a "Top Harness" it worked just fine for me and wearing it under my jeans gave my crotch a very noticeable bulge. Once Gary saw that he became more interested in spending time with me.

I don't remember if he and I ever actually ended up in bed but I know we played with a pair of handcuffs and rope a few times. The whole idea of getting a guy tied up was still working really well for me, but something was missing.

Outside the leather bar, I had little contact with others in the community. It was still a hidden subculture at that time, so the bars were the main meeting places. I did manage to find a few partners who enjoyed bondage and some spankings, and those sessions usually ended in a hot night of rough sex. However, I didn't have any serious relationships with anyone from the leather scene.

What I did learn was that I wanted more. I saw guys play at the bar out in the patio after hours, and I watched a few flogging scenes done as part of a contest for a leather title, but I had never done any of it myself. Finally I got the nerve to start asking questions and I found the other Tops in the bar were more than happy to give me advice. They looked sever and imposing, but underneath they were just guys who enjoyed their sex rough and their men masculine.

I got tips on how to tell when a bottom had had enough, instructions on where you could hit with a flogger and where you couldn't. I even learned a few rope ties and bondage tips and before long I changed the color of my hanky to black. A black hanky meant you were into SM and I wanted to do the real thing. Genuine full blown SM was calling me and I surrendered to it.

Unlike many guys who came into the scene as a bottom and finally settled as a Top, I started as a Top in training. Through the years I have experienced just about everything imaginable in the SM arena, and I do not like to do anything to a bottom I haven't felt myself, but I don't consider myself ever having been a bottom or a switch. I am a Top with an appreciation of the effects of pain and bondage. It is my personal belief that if you have never felt a particular SM activity, you have no business doing it to someone else.

I also found a camaraderie in the leather community that was unlike any place else. The leathermen who were my early mentors accepted me for who I was. I didn't have to be drop dead gorgeous, a great dancer, have a huge cock or be anything other than myself. As I grew in the scene and learned more I found my status was based on my experience. Those who were older and more skilled were more revered, and I liked that kind of structure.

There was a civilized protocol to the leather scene. Respect, honor and manners seemed to really matter and there was a lot less gossip than in the gay community in general. I liked that, too. I remember the training my parents instilled in me as a child. They taught me how to behave in a formal atmosphere, how to address people politely and how to interact in a civil way with others. In the leather community all that training came in handy, and I fit in as comfortably as many of the leathermen who came from a military background.

Though I had been a part of the "love generation", I still liked things to have a structure, and though my sexual preferences were decidedly rebellious, I enjoyed the civilized culture of leather. I was finding a home in the leather community, one that has nurtured and guided my life more than I ever expected.

Today, our community still exists though the advent of the Internet has made it far more accessible than ever. There are good and bad aspects to this modern version of the leather community. The good is the ease with which people can get information about us and our activities. The bad is that the accuracy of that information is often questionable and many times just plain wrong.

The ease of finding the community online should not be confused with the actual becoming part of that community. Though anyone can probably find a leather club or BDSM social event, and call themselves whatever they wish, be it "Master of the Universe" or just the ubiquitous "kajira", it takes a while to really fit in and find a place.

We are eager to accept people in the modern leather community, since in so many ways we have been turned away because of our kink, however just being accepted should not be confused with being part of the community. That takes time, work and a willingness to serve the greater good of everyone involved. That part is often missed by newcomers, and without it leather/BDSM/fetish people are just a collection of individuals with their own agenda, not a community.

I found it surprising that once I had begun to learn about the early Christian community I found the same principals applied. Though the first disciples were a band of misfits and outcasts, they gave up everything and bonded together for the common good. It is a very good model for how to build a community.

I look back on that time when I first came into the community. I did it through that bar, and it was a journey that has helped shape who I am. You see, when I got the courage to go into that bar the first time I didn't go as a tourist. Lots of gay men go to leather bars to see the sights. It's exciting to see men who wrap themselves in the look and feel of hyper-masculinity that goes hand in hand with leather. These visitors come to look and ogle the hides and flesh. They are titillated by the thought of men openly wearing their fetish and the sexually charged atmosphere of the place. These visitors are sexual tourists. They come to see the sights, but not to really participate in the culture. Like a busload of camera toting sightseers, they are voyeurs whose thrill comes from seeing a foreign place and its colorful customs.

When I came into the leather bar, I was driven by some of the same curiosity, but I came more as a pilgrim. I knew there was something I wanted in that place. It was something beyond the momentary turn-on of seeing all the leathermen. I was drawn to it because I knew there was something there that was already part of me. I went to the leather bar to claim the sexuality that had been growing in me since I was a teenager. I came to hear, see and learn the language of leather. It scared me and it seduced me.

Leather, is something deep in my soul. Yes, it is a fetish. I like wearing leather. I like the feel, the smell, the way it clings to me like a second skin. I also like the way it speaks. Leather on a kinky person like me, makes a statement. It says I enjoy a sexual ethos that is on the fringes of traditional society. I am a sexual pioneer, an explorer in the realm of the sensual and erotic.

Leather says I value traditions. Not just any traditions, but those of my own community. Our stories, our lives all speak in the language of leather. It speaks of respect for those who came before me and for those just learning the ropes. Leather speaks of respect for all human beings and the ability to honor their abilities and peculiarities. Leather speaks of energy and power. It tells of the primal forces of the animals from which it came and of the mysterious power exchange that is key to my sexual identity.

Leather, for me, is not a lifestyle, it is part of my life, and because of that I find it difficult to separate it from my spirituality, my religion and my God.

Leather Sacraments

That first entry into a leather bar was a rite of passage. Just as my Bar Mitzvah initiated me into the Temple as a teenager, walking in the door of Sundance Kids started my initiation into the leather community, but there were many more steps to take before I could become a part of this tribe. One of the first was getting a true understanding of what leathermen did that was different than other gay men.

The clothing and accessories were the most obvious differences. My first leather bar had a dress code, which meant if you weren't wearing leather, a jacket, vest, chaps, pants or a shirt, then you were not welcome. Jeans and boots would do if you took off your shirt, but I didn't have a shirtless body, and I still don't. Luckily, I already owned the beginnings of a leatherman's wardrobe. My motorcycle jacket and harness boots bought me admittance to the place.

Today there are not many bars that have a dress code. I suspect there are lots of problems with discrimination that could be raised because of dress codes, but something has been lost that in my opinion surpasses discrimination. The open wearing of the fetish of leather in a bar or dungeon gives the place a sense of being special. It's a visceral thing, that sight of so many men and women in leather or fetish wear. It's just sexy, and I miss that. Walk into most leather bars today and you'll see anything from old guard outfits to guys in Bermuda shorts and polo shirts. It may be comfortable, but it's not what attracted me to the leather bar and I doubt that I would have had the same fascination with the place today.

Getting beyond the outer manifestations of leatherfolk, I was soon to learn what went on beneath that second skin. It didn't happen quickly. I didn't have the internet where I could look it up. I had to do some digging. The first place I dug was in the local gay bookstore. There I found lots of magazines that showed guys in leather. So, I bought them. Lots of them!

These magazines were full of men having sex in leather. That was enough for a while, but I got the sense that there was more to it than that. Oh the visuals were a turn on and I spent many nights fantasizing with those magazines, but I had more than a leather fetish. That's when I found Larry Townsend's *Leatherman's Handbook*. That book was an eye opener. It contained the "it" that I had been looking for.

"It" was SM, and that book along with the now defunct *Drummer Magazine* began to give me some solid information about what leathermen actually did. I was fascinated by it all. The rope bondage, the flogging, and especially what seemed at the time a rather specialized practice of CBT (cock and ball torture). The information in that book and the magazines showed me a whole new world. And in *Drummer* there were photos. Actual photos of men doing SM!

Again, the magazines served to stoke my fantasies, but more importantly they were educating me. They were showing me what could be done in the realm of sex that I had never imagined. This all happened around the same time I first started going into the leather bars and the stories I heard from the leathermen there and the material I was reading got the ball rolling for me. Before long I wanted to get some hands-on experience. That would take a while.

There were no public play spaces or dungeons then in Dallas.

Most BDSM play took place in the privacy of people's bedrooms or at small private parties. I was still too green to get an invitation to these, but I did get invited to various leathermen's homes for casual socialization.

On the coffee table was a photo album. It was the kind you might expect to find wedding pictures or snapshots of the grandkids in. Opening it I found something very different. That is where I saw my first pictures from Inferno. The Chicago Hellfire Club holds an invitation only event every year called Inferno at a secret location. Getting an invitation to one of these events is a big deal, and because of that people who attended brought back souvenirs. The photos were just such a souvenir.

There were pictures of men doing the things I had read about in *The Leatherman's Handbook* and *Drummer* and things I had never imagined possible. I found pictures of men in what looked like extreme pain, their faces contorted in obvious agony. Just a few photos later, there were the same men, sometimes with bloody marks on their backs, smiling and laughing. I could not take my eyes off them.

My host explained that the event was perhaps the most extreme SM "run" in the country, so when you went there you wanted to experience things you couldn't do anywhere else. From the photos I knew he was right. That's when I came to the photo of my host, lying in a sling with another man's hand inserted deep in his ass. I had heard about fisting but had never seen it before and it transfixed me.

My host laughed and said with a little hint of embarrassment, "I was certainly being a little piggy that day."

I laughed nervously and agreed, not really understanding what the activity was all about. It would be a couple of years before I saw it in person at a notorious bar in New York called the Mineshaft.

He then explained that he was really into ass-play. I nodded as though I knew all about it and tried not to flinch when he pulled out a large chrome ball from the drawer in the table.

"This is my favorite," he said handing the ball to me. "It weighs about a pound."

I nodded and hefted the steel ball in my hand. It was heavy and large and before I knew it I was in his bedroom where he was instructing me in the application of Crisco to his butt. With coaching from him I managed to slip the large sphere into his ass. It was like a strange magic trick. Presto! Gone!

At his urging I followed that little trick with a good firm spanking. I noticed he seemed really turned on by that. His backside was soon rosy pink and my hand and crotch were tingling from the activity.

Not long afterward, he was nuzzling my boots and crotch. My first topping experience with a piggy bottom was happening so fast it caught me by surprise, and that afternoon I found that I really liked it.

My host licked my boots clean and I rewarded him with a nice long session doing the same to my penis. He called me "Sir" and I took easily to the title. I was soon ordering him around much to his delight. That simple play drew me into an intimacy that few people ever experience. Later we shared a cup of coffee and a joint.

What transpired between us was a "scene". It was not the beginning of a relationship, just a phase in a casual friendship and my initiation as a Top. It was mild compared to what I do today, but everyone has to start somewhere. That night I went home and played the events over and over in my head. It was as if I had suddenly become part of one of the photos that were so exciting in the pictures of Inferno. I really liked "it", and there was no going back.

I still remember that afternoon and that photo album and I understand how important they were. I finally did get an invitation to Inferno, 12 years later. Today I look at my own photos from those events and realize they are very much a family album, and Inferno is sort of a family reunion. I only wish I had more pictures, since many if not all of the people from my early years in the leather community are gone.

Missing In Action

As I noted earlier, around 1980 I met and moved in with a charming man who wanted to be my "boy". David (not his real name) was a quick witted and spunky guy with a bushy head of curly hair. We met at an organizing meeting for the Gay Pride Parade, and hit it off immediately. Since we both were wearing leather that evening, it seemed obvious that we would find common ground. We were actually introduced by a lesbian friend of mine. She was sort of the Dolly Levi of the city's gay and lesbian community and later I found she sometimes ran with the local leather dykes.

After a brief courtship, I asked David to move in with me in high-rise apartment near the center of gay life in Dallas. We got along pretty well, and I liked it when we played with the various restraints and chains attached to my big bed. David wore lots of leather and chain jewelry, and he had an affinity for punk fashion that meshed well with the leather fetish styles.

That same year we met Frank and Carmen. These two older leathermen became my mentors and it was their patient coaching that got me through the first difficult years in the community. David and I began exploring more and more BDSM activities and at Frank's urging attended a couple of Dallas Motorcycle Club events. DMC was primarily a bike club, but most of the members at that time were involved in the BDSM world as well. Eventually, though we didn't have motorcycles, we pledged as members and since I had a van, we became valuable additions for the club functions and runs.

Most of the activities of the DMC were centered on the bar, in this case the Hidden Door, another local leather bar, but far less intimidating than the Sundance Kids. It was a neighborhood bar with a leather twist. Our club held bar nights every month and as a pledge I ended up tending bar a lot. That gave me the opportunity to meet and chat with even more leathermen than before. The following fall, David and I spent a couple of weekends down at the farm of one of our members, cleaning the brush away and preparing for the club's annual run.

That event was the first time I actually got to play with other leathermen outdoors. That was glorious. Late nights here was a special area a few hundred feet from the main campground where members had set up St. Andrew's crosses and a few other pieces of equipment. There during the wee hours of the night, we held our own version of the events that went on at Inferno. Though things never got too intense, it did allow me to learn a few lessons and see my first scene involving a single tail or bullwhip. That was an eye opener!

That event and several other ones like it really gave me and David a chance to experience what "real" leathermen did. I really liked it, but for David it was different. One night after I tied him up in preparation for a play scene, I left to make a quick trip to the bathroom and when I returned found him sitting on the bed holding the ropes.

"You are going to have to do a lot better than that if you want to hold me." David said with a grin.

I took the challenge and tied him up again, this time more elaborately, but still not so tight as to cut off circulation in any of his extremities. Before I could finish he was struggling and slipping out of the bonds. For David this was becoming an escape act, not a BDSM scene.

I guess I was not seasoned enough to know how to handle his rowdiness and I finally gave up.

He finished untying his bonds and tossed them to me.

"You know," David said, "this is all just theatre. It just doesn't work for me."

That evening was not one of my highpoints. I think we talked about it some more, but eventually he made it clear that leather was just a passing interest for him and he preferred more vanilla activities in the bedroom. After a discussion I acquiesced and we limited out leather to a fashion statement rather than the BDSM realm.

I began seeking my leather play elsewhere. I joined a secret local club that was tucked away in the back of a newsstand. The old house, now converted into a business, had lots of small rooms and corridors that wound around like a maze. It was dimly lit but that was no problem. More importantly some rooms contained what I would now call play areas. There was a room with a couple of slings, another with a St. Andrew's Cross and a room with a big bathtub in the center. Though I didn't visit the place very often, the times I did were usually highlighted with at least one encounter that would qualify as SM. That club, called the DEN, for Dallas Evening News, closed after only a few months in operation, so my BDSM play was pretty much curtailed.

The following year we bought a house in the suburbs and moved out of the gay neighborhood. We started living like more conventional folks, with a couple of dogs in the yard and a well decorated house that we used to entertain my business associates and David's friends. That year I lost touch with the leather community, and a part of my life was put on hold, for a while.

While we still remained active in the political life of the community,

David considered the leather/BDSM/fetish subculture not very politically correct. I was too involved in the political struggle to put much effort into disagreeing and since the only time we spent with anyone from the gay community was in meetings or rallies, we hardly noticed when several leathermen became very ill and died. Sometime in 1981 I heard the term GRID (Gay Related Immune Disorder) a syndrome that would later be christened AIDS.

The leather community in Dallas caught the first wave of the AIDS epidemic and it hit hard. By the mid 1980's many of the people who had ushered me into the leather community were dead, and worse, I didn't even know it until I read the obituaries in the local gay newspaper.

I got a call from my mentor Carmen once afternoon. Frank had gotten out of the hospital and he wanted to get together with me and David for dinner. I was shocked. I didn't even know Frank was sick. That dinner was the last time I saw Frank alive. He had been a robust older leather daddy with a thick grey moustache and scruffy beard. The man I saw at dinner was a stranger. He was thin and frail and clean shaven. That night I went home and wept.

About a month later I got a call from Carmen. Frank had died. He told me when the funeral was and I made plans to attend. It was the first of many funerals I went to, but there were many more I missed. Being isolated in the suburbs, I lost touch with the leather community. I will always miss those guys who were such an important part of my life at the time, and I will always regret not being able to wish them farewell in their journey from this world.

Isolating in the wilds of North Dallas was both bad and good. Since my circle of friends changed almost completely, I lost touch with the first people struck by the AIDS epidemic, the leather community. If anything good came from it, it was my isolation. That isolation may have saved me from becoming infected right when the disease was at its most virulent. My sex life had become monogamous and once I understood how HIV was spread, I became obsessed with safe sex.

I will not claim that God spared me from the epidemic, but I am grateful that I have survived until now when so many of my friends are gone.

It was only six or seven months later that I got a call from Carmen. He was in the hospital and I went to visit him. I poked my head into his room, but didn't recognize the thin youngish looking man in the bed, so I went back to the nurses' station to inquire if I had made a mistake. Before I could get there I heard Carmen's voice.

"Hey, you call that a visit?"

I turned and looked at the thin guy standing at the door of his room. He looked almost childlike but soon Carmen's familiar features melted through the façade. He had shaved, and since I had never seen him without a beard it was a surprise anyway, but Carmen was always a big bear of a man, and seeing him so thin really must have put a shocked look on my face.

"Yea," he said, "It's me. Damn lousy way to go on a diet though."

I laughed and walked toward him. I was met with a gentle hug, and I returned it with the same care, fearing I might break the frail man in my embrace.

"So how are you doing?" I mumbled.

"I have good days and bad," Carmen replied. "Mostly bad, lately."

We continued the small talk as I walked him back to his bed. He had lots of flowers in the room from his business associates and friends. None were from me. The guilt was starting to hit me hard. I had lost touch with Carmen, and only reestablished contact now that it was too late to help out or to really be much of a friend.

That didn't matter to him. He was glad to see me and he took up right where our friendship left off. We talked about business, friends and leather. I asked how he was getting by at home alone and he told me how the people in his church had been helping out. The idea that Carmen went to church surprised me, since he had never talked about it before.

"I never took you for church people." I said.

"Well, Frank had always gone to the Episcopal Church, and raised Catholic; it wasn't much of a leap for me to attend with him."

"The church ladies must have had a shock when they came over to your house." I smiled, remembering the multitude of leather toys and photos of leather events that decorated the couple's apartment.

"Oh, I had a couple of friends help me hide most of that." Carmen said sheepishly.

I simply nodded in agreement, knowing how difficult taking down all their memories must have been.

We chatted for about an hour until his nurse arrived with the evening medication. I bid him farewell and promised to visit again the following week. As I kissed him and left his room, I had a sinking feeling that next week might be too late. I was right.

Carmen's funeral was held out of town, near his parent's home in Massachusetts. Luckily, he was buried near Frank as far as I know. I never got a chance to speak to him again before he died, but I learned something very valuable from our brief visit. I would never again let a friend slip away without knowing it. I would never again turn my back on people who made such a big difference in my life. Though I had left the leather community, leather had not left me.

The other thing I learned was that though Carmen's church was very supportive and loving, apparently that love had a limit. Leather seemed to be an aspect of his life that he was either hesitant to share with his church or they were unwilling to understand. That lesson stuck with me and later became a litmus test for any religious affiliation. If I was going to ever be part of a church again, it would have to accept me for who I was - all of who I was.

Spiritual Wandering

Over the years I have made many friends in the leather/BDSM/fetish community. Of all these folks only a small number have ever professed to be in any way religious, though many freely speak of their spirituality. Many of them have had bad experiences with religion and walked away from it rather than trying to reconcile with it. I understand this fully. I did the same thing not long after the death of my father.

I think it was not so much a reaction to that event as it was an unspoken feeling that my religion wouldn't like the person I really was if they knew. Few religions accepted gay people back in the 1960's, and though I didn't officially come out until a few years later, I felt pretty sure my sexual tendencies would be met with condemnation.

In reality, I never looked into it. I just made the assumption and figured I could avoid the rejection by simply avoiding the issue. As I mentioned earlier, attending Baylor, even as a secular Jew was an eye opener. I got a taste of the Baptist religion and was not impressed with either the theology or the adherents to it. At the time the concept of Biblical Inerrancy was just starting to make resurgence and having read the bible in my religious school classes as a pre-teenager, I immediately figured that these folks must be reading a different book.

Literalism like fundamentalism requires an intellectual disconnect that I just couldn't manage. The stories in the Bible were obviously, in my opinion, compiled from an earlier oral tradition and were meant to convey big concepts not minutia. Unfortunately, the literalists cannot see the big concepts of the forest for the minutia of the trees. They seemed to spend all their time looking for a secret formula or rules that would assure them of some kind of reward in the afterlife rather than living in this one. Along the way, they seemed intent on making everyone else's life a living hell.

That impression is still one that I find valid, though it was first formed by the endless visits from well meaning students, who made me their project at Baylor. It seems that conversion is vital for them to feel like they are practicing their religion. The problem is that it meddles in the lives and happiness of folks like me, who wanted no part of it, but were too polite to scream at them. I also found that these people lived in constant fear. They were afraid of straying from the path of righteousness, and that path was a strict one.

No drinking, no smoking, no dancing, no drugs, were only the first four items on a long list of forbidden pleasures that were unavailable to the Baptists I met at Baylor. The biggest problem I had was that for such a righteous place, the university when I attended it had the largest number of unwed pregnancies in the Southwest Conference, a group of schools that included the University of Texas, Oklahoma University and Arkansas State. Something seemed really wrong here.

So from my university experience I figured most Christians were like the Baptists I had met and wanted no part of them. I didn't turn back toward Christianity for almost 25 years. Yet I still felt a need to connect with something bigger than myself, and that longing stayed with me for many years.

When I returned to Dallas, to attend the local community college, I decided to sample the spiritual smorgasbord that had sprung up in the 60's. I had friends who practiced something they called Wicca, and I thought it sounded interesting. Since I had been a magician of the sleight of hand variety, the idea of magic didn't seem too farfetched, especially since I had tried a few mind altering drugs that worked like magic to transport me to other realms of reality. At least that is how it seemed at the time. I suspect the fact that I was sniffing incense and listening to the Jefferson Airplane at the time may have helped.

The people I hung out with were not strict Wiccan, instead they followed something called the Daughters of Isis, and though I never got a full indoctrination into the practice, it did involve a lot of "natural spirits". Everything in nature had a spiritual component to them and I felt there might have been something to it. I attended a few of their gatherings and found them very friendly and accepting of everyone.

Being attracted to someone of the same sex was no problem with them; in fact they considered it somewhat sacred. I liked that. Some of these people also practiced a kind of neo-spiritualism where they attempted to contact the dead and spirit guides from beyond this world. I also liked this because the Ouija board had been one of my favorite gadgets as a teenager.

I liked the ritualistic part of these folks practice, but in the end I had a lot of trouble with the basic tenants of the beliefs. Still I can see how nature religions could be attractive to others, especially to leatherfolk who may have found their practices far too outside the mainstream to be accepted in the faith of their childhood. Baptists in particular seemed to look down on the pleasures of the flesh, but the Wiccans and Daughters of Isis I met reveled in them. In fact they seemed to fully embrace sex as a sacred part of their life. What's not to like about that?

Some of these people even called themselves witches and warlocks. The made potions and chanted spells and cast circles. It was all very dramatic and that was the part I like. For a time I even had my own tools of art, the knife or anthame, a chalice and other materials that cluttered up my bedroom. My herb and ingredient collection got a bit out of hand, but did come in handy when my mother ran out of spices.

About this time I began really exploring my sexuality and the faith quest was soon left by the wayside in favor of another quest. I wanted sex, lots of it and with anyone who was amenable to it. I dated women and men and sometimes both at the same time. It was the "love generation" after all and I intended to get my share of that.

It was during this period that I first found the gay scene. I visited a few gay bars and found the people there to be friendly if not a little bit too feminine for my tastes. Still the drag shows were fun and I met a lot of people who would become close friends. It was also where I developed my taste for activism and politics.

The bars in Dallas when I first came out were subject to frequent raids by the police. Dancing with members of the same sex was illegal, and cross-dressing was looked on as a vice. It was not uncommon to be dancing in a nightclub when the lights flashed. That was the signal to stop dancing with another man find a handy lesbian or just start milling around.

The vice squad pushed their way through the bars on a regular basis, and I consider myself lucky not to have been arrested. It was that kind of harassment that led me to join the fledgling Dallas Gay Political Caucus. This newly formed group was attempting to bring together gay men and women to foster change in the way gay people were treated. These folks were doing something about it, not just whining about the injustice and I liked that a lot.

The DGPC crowd was also a lot more diverse than the bar crowd. Men and women of every age were starting to come out and try to form a cohesive political power base. We met at a church, and that's where I was first exposed to the Metropolitan Community Church, the first predominately gay and lesbian denomination.

Walking into those DGPC meetings was always uncomfortable for me. There was the pulpit and the cross on the wall behind it. It brought back all the memories of those bad times at Baylor, and though MCC was certainly not Baptist the church could have passed for one with the exception of a Baptismal pool.

The local MCC pastor was a member of the DGPC and I got to know him socially. He seemed like a pretty nice guy and so I decided to try out one of the Sunday services. For me that was a mistake. Though the congregation was filled with some of the same folks who I worked with in the caucus, it also had a large number of people who I had never seen, and with the exception of their sexual orientation, they acted a lot like the Baylor crowd.

When shouts of "Amen" and "Praise Jesus" erupted from the congregation spontaneously during the sermon, I started looking for the door. Before the service was over, I had inched my way toward the exit and when one drag queen in the back began waving her white handkerchief during the upbeat hymn, I snuck out.

Interestingly, the Universal Fellowship of Metropolitan Community Churches was founded by Reverend Troy Perry. He felt the need for a church that not only accepted gay, lesbian, bisexual and transgendered people, but celebrated them. More interestingly, Rev. Perry is a leatherman. He has spoken at many leather/BDSM events and though we are not close friends, he has given me occasional personal advice. I did not learn of his leather affiliation until much later in my life, or else I might have stuck it out at that first MCC service.

I know now that this Pentecostal flavor of the service was typical for some MCC churches but not others. At the time, I had nothing to compare it to, so I decided to steer clear of the church except for political gatherings. Around this time, I had also begin my relationship with David and he was a non practicing Catholic who wanted nothing to do with the church in any form. So my spiritual quest moved from church to a more personal journey.

As I mentioned earlier I am a recovering addict and an Al-Anon. I found that program while in my relationship with David. In fact he guided me to it after his own recovery began. David had been attending AA meetings for several weeks, and I suppose he got tired of me asking him what went on there. He told me they had a special meeting for the significant others of alcoholics and maybe I would like attending that meeting while he was in his meeting at AA.

I accepted his offer and walked into my first AL-Anon meeting in 1986. I found so much there, it would take a book of its own, but the most important thing that came from it was a real understanding of my higher power. With the help of a sponsor who had the patience of a saint, I worked my way through the 12 steps. Because of my new found serenity and David's sobriety, we both become more open to resuming our spiritual journeys.

We both ended up at the Unitarian Universalist Church. This very old denomination was a very liberal one, and though it was not a Christian church in the strictest sense, its services felt more structured than any I had found so far. I liked it and became comfortable there. Eventually I joined the First Unitarian Church of Dallas and even became active in the church activities. Unitarians love activities!

That church was instrumental in the movement that led to Roe vs. Wade and he congregation was filled with politically activists. These were my kind of folks, who put their moral and ethical beliefs to work. As my contribution, I produced a film for the congregation that served as a newcomers guide for many years. This was one of the first churches I felt really comfortable in. I would probably still be there had not David and I separated a few years after joining.

My only problem with the Unitarians was what I perceived as a lack of an anchor. Now I don't want this to come across as over critical, because I dearly love the Unitarian Universalists. This is about me, and my need for something concrete to hang my beliefs on. The Unitarians were very enlightened and moral folks, their faith is about the dignity of the individual and a justice-centered belief system. For me what was missing was something more concrete. I met people who attended the

Unitarian church who considered themselves agnostic, pagans and even atheists and I loved them all, however I wanted more. I wanted a religion that had a more defined relationship with God.

After a few more years of wandering I would find that religion and reclaim my leather soul in the process.

Born Again as a Leatherman

As I said before, David and I spit amicably and with that separation I severed my relationship with the Unitarian Universalists. That was as painful as leaving David, but I managed to accept it. I kept working my 12 step program and going to meetings. I started getting involved in politics again and even began spending time back in the gay "hood" of Dallas.

During this time I had opened a successful film production company that focused on commercial productions and industrial documentaries. My business kept me so busy that my sex life was practically non-existent. That wouldn't last for long.

One day when I was cleaning out my closet, an activity that I do not believe I have done since, my leather motorcycle cap fell from the top shelf into my hands. I hadn't seen it in years and coming into contact with it sent a flood of feelings coursing through me. I carefully cleaned the dust and a little mold off it and the stepped into the bathroom. As I watched myself in the mirror, I put the cap on and at that moment I realized what I had forgotten.

The sights and sounds of the Sundance Kids came rushing in. The feel of a tight leather harness pressed against my skin. My nostrils were filled with the smell the cigars I used to smoke. The friends who I would never see again were gathered around me. I stood there looking at the leatherman in the mirror and I wept. Why had I ever stepped away from that part of my life?

A few nights later, I went down to the building where the Sundance Kids used to be. It was empty, but the large warehouse next door was bustling. I made my way into The Brick Bar, and unlike the first time I walked into a leather bar, I felt right at home.

Grabbing a bottle of Calistoga Mineral Water from the bar I walked around the busy club. This leather bar had a dance floor, and watching leather men and women dance was something new for me. I liked it too. Gone was the stoic posturing along the bar and what replaced it was a more energetic paradigm. People were friendlier, yet there was still the unmistakable feeling of a leather bar. I leaned against the rail around the dance floor and watched for a while then went out to the patio for a cigar. As I was about to light up, a very good looking leatherman offered me a light. He was the doorman for the bar and was on break. We struck up a conversation that eventually led to a strong friendship. John was not only the doorman, but he served as the club's auditor and bookkeeper during the day.

He was a perfect contact for me to reestablish my presence in the leather community. John knew everyone, and he introduced me to a group of people who to this day are some of my closest friends. Through that network, I eventually found my way to the local chapter of the National Leather Association. That organization was only a few members at the time, but it was a good place to make connections with real leatherfolk again.

Through my contacts there I found a small play group called Leather Rose Society. This was a primarily heterosexual group, but they welcomed me with open arms. Headed up my Michelle and her husband Rick this club was a great place to play. The dungeon was her garage basement, and there were few amenities other than the basics of a St. Andrews Cross and a couple of benches, but it was filled with people who were as passionate about leather and BDSM as I was. It was a great place to get back on the path that I had abandoned for those years I spent in suburbia.

I quickly immersed myself in the community and though it had started to change, there were a few "old guard" folks still around. Surprisingly, I found myself included in this number by most of the people I came in contact with. "New Leather" was staring to appear. It was a combination of retro-punk fashion and science fiction/fantasy. Most of the folks involved were heterosexual or bisexual, but they could still be recognized as leatherfolk. The surface may have been different but their hearts were still kinky and we got along well.

Additionally, these people wanted to talk to me. They figured since I had been around longer than they had I might be able to contribute to their knowledge. It didn't take long to see where this new leather was a lot like old leather. There was a respect for experience and a willingness to learn.

As I became involved with the National Leather Association, I began to meet more gay leathermen and women. These were a combination of survivors of the 1980's like me and newcomers who had found the community through books and computer bulletin boards. These crude precursors to the chat rooms of the World Wide Web still provided a point of contact for someone who knew they wanted "it" but were still unsure what "it" was. Sound familiar?

I made many good friends during that second coming out into leather. Most of them are still my friends today. I gained a new understanding of the many faces of the leather community. One of my dearest friends is a feisty red haired leather dyke who really stretched my preconceived notions a lot. She had a gay man in service to her. Her boy was a striking blond guy a couple of feet taller than her and it took me several months to really understand their relationship.

That was the first time I really got the DS part of the BDSM equation. DS can stand for dominance and submission, and it is a delightful kind of role-play that Ms T and her boy really got into. To watch them together you instantly realized the elegant power exchange that went on. It was almost like watching dancers. He, always in a position of submission to her, yet attentive and constantly watching her every move. She, moving with a seemingly effortless grace yet still sending him signals and cues as to what behavior was expected from him.

My experiences in those early days of my reawakening into leather were among some of the fondest memories I have. Indirectly they also led me to meet the man I would spend the rest of my life with.

In my professional life, my business was doing well and as a commercial producer and director I kept my days busy with creating 30 second masterpieces that were designed to move product. They were fun but not really creatively fulfilling. I still longed to do something serious that would validate me as a filmmaker.

Meanwhile, one of my friends in Al-Anon was heading up the first Gay and Lesbian Film Festival in Dallas. It was coming up in three months, and so I asked her if I could still submit a short film for consideration. She was delighted to hear I was interested and gave me her assurance it would be considered for the festival.

It was that idea that helped my filmmaking and leather life converge. I had written a book of poetry several years before my brief sabbatical from leather and though I never published it, I felt there was some merit to the work. I conceived an idea based on one of the poems and decided to create a short film that would be in essence a film-poem. In just a few days I was starting to work on "Leather" the short film I intended to submit to the festival.

I had long felt that previous depictions of SM had missed the eroticism and beauty of the gay leather scene. When I say beauty, I am not talking about the kind of videos that have flooded the market with lots of hunky guys and graphic sex, but very little leather eroticism. I decided to create visual imagery that spoke of the raw power and sensuality of SM and leather. Using my contacts in the film community, I recruited a cameraman, production manager, grips and lighting technicians who worked for free or at cost on the project.

Within the group of new found friends I recruited my cast. Working whenever people were available, we shot mostly at night using the studio space behind my office. We shot for several nights creating scenes that would illustrate the words of the poem that acted as the shooting script of the film.

Everyone in the film was actually in the leather scene, there were no actors, and the footage we produced was strikingly beautiful. Shot in black & white, on 16mm film the light and shadow of the images went well with the black leather most of the participants wore. By the time I had finished the first weeks shooting I knew I had a good film.

I decided to add interviews with some of my friends to augment the narration that my poem would provide. I am grateful that I did that, because several of the people in the film are no longer around and those interviews area testament to their leather history. I shot these on video, since I couldn't afford a sound recordist and at that time most professional video cameras recorded sound and picture at the same time. I then took the video and played the edited interviews back through a monitor and shot this with a 16mm film camera in order to degrade the images into a gritty, flicker color image. I wanted these to have a "live" quality and the play to have a lyric fantasy quality. The final product worked well.

I got a friends band to do the ethereal score and in a few weeks the project was finished and ready for the festival. I finished "Leather" just 2 days before the festival and luckily they accepted it with open arms. The night of the showing, NLA-Dallas invited all their members to the premier, and I was even asked to speak for a few minutes after the showing.

It was an exciting time for me, and the film though short was very well received. Afterward as I answered questions, I quipped that making the film was a good way to get a date, and I was available. Little did I know that quip would be the catalyst for meeting the man who has become my boy and the love of my life.

Patrick walked down the aisle of the theatre after the festival and approached me very politely. "Sir," he said, "were you serious about being available?"

I smiled back at the handsome bearded redhead who stood before me. "Why yes, I was."

After a few more words, we ended up agreeing to go out for a bite to eat after the festival. It was around 11:00pm and we traveled up to a local Brazilian coffee shop for a late night breakfast. He followed me on his Harley Davidson. I liked him immediately.

We spent the next couple of hours chatting and laughing, then around 1:00am I asked him if he wanted to go over to my house. He did, and that night, though we did a lot of kissing, we ended up sleeping until late in the morning. The next morning we played and had more conventional sex as well. That pattern has stayed with us until this day. We are both morning people I guess.

After dating for several weeks, I finally asked him and his delightful cat Opus to move in with me and he agreed. Since then Patrick and I have been together and on the whole very happy. It was his arrival that led me to the spiritual and church home I have today. It was through Patrick and his friends that I met my first Christian Leathermen, and that would in turn lead me to baptism in the church.

Like a Voice Shouting in the Wilderness

It was a Sunday afternoon, and he Texas spring was being unusually kind. No storms on the horizon and a balmy 80 degrees with a slight breeze. Patrick and I pulled up to the small brick house and walked up to the door. In side I could hear laughter and men's voices. If I hadn't known what kind of group I was visiting, I would have assumed it was just another gay social group meeting for food and camaraderie. In some ways it was pretty ordinary, with the exception of what some of the men wore; it could have been just any gathering of gay men. Instead, this was a group of leathermen, and their purpose was to socialize and talk about their spirituality and the Bible.

Several of the guys I met that day I had seen out in the community and a few I had not. All of them were friendly and easy to talk to. Once we had chatted a bit and filled ourselves on the potluck luncheon that was provided we sat down in a circle to begin the discussion in earnest. The leader of the group was Jackson Myer, a respected member of the leather community and a titleholder of some regional leather contest. He began the "meeting" part of the afternoon with a short prayer and then passed out the study plan for the afternoon.

I had never attended a "bible study" group so the whole thing was new to me. Luckily, the section of the scripture they were going to discuss was the story of Jonathan and David from the book of Samuel. I knew this story since it was one of the ones we covered in my classes in religious school. We learned it as a tale of friendship and valor, but it had been years since I read it. As the lesson continued we read again that story, but now, as a mature gay man I was struck by the not so subtle subtext of the tale. Jonathan and David were not just good friends, they were lovers.

It didn't take a scholar to get the gist of the emphatic statement, "Jonathan and David made a covenant, because he loved him as his own soul". That is more than just friendship, and when later in the story when it notes, "And Jonathan stripped himself of the robe that was upon him, and gave it to David, and his garments, even to his sword, and to his bow, and to his girdle", the connotation is even more obvious. I had always read the Bible as some sort of quasi-historical book and never looked for gays and lesbians in it.

Before the meeting was over, we had a lively discussion of the gay and lesbian characters in the Bible, from Ruth and Naomi to the story of the centurion in the New Testament who loved his slave so much that he asked Jesus to heal him. Many of the stories had no outright homosexual characters, but when read with a gay sensibility; they leapt off the page and out of the Biblical closet.

After the meeting, I stayed and chatted with Jackson and his partner Roger for a while. They were really engaging men and seemed to have a good grasp of reality as well as a profound spiritual bent. It would only be a few months later when I would be asked to step in and take over this group, but at the time that was the furthest thing from my mind.

The following Sunday I went to church with Patrick. It was a big step for me since he attended the MCC in Dallas. I attended half expecting to find the same Pentecostal flavored worship service, but figured if it was important to Patrick I would go along. The Cathedral of Hope as the church was now called had just finished their new building a couple of years earlier. The place was big and bright and welcoming.

We arrived just as the service was starting and took a place in the back of the church. Both Patrick and I wore dress shirts with our leather vests over them. I had been told at the bible study group that leather was acceptable in the congregation. I also felt that church was a special place, and as such wearing special clothes made sense. For me as a leatherman, wearing my leather, with the front of my vest regaled with run pins and badges was as close to formal wear as I could imagine. To my relief, no one seemed to be surprised.

That first service was interesting. There were over 800 people present and the pews were filled as well as temporary seats at the rear. It was a long way from the Metropolitan Community Church I remembered from my past. The service was what I would call "high church" with lots of pageantry and the clergy wearing clerical robes with brightly decorated stoles. Surprisingly, that made me comfortable. My childhood church, Temple Emanuel, had a similar feel. Lots of music and a compliment of rabbis dressed in long robes with prayer shawls. The difference here was that the music was provided by a full orchestra and a very large choir.

My friend Jackson was directing the choir and I recognized the organist as a leatherman I knew from the bar scene. Though they were in suits, their close cropped hair and drooping moustaches were unmistakable. This was going to be interesting indeed.

The first strains of the processional started and we rose to our feet. As the orchestra and organ built to a triumphant introduction the choir began singing as did everyone around me. I didn't know the words, but the music was very familiar. It was a melody by Joseph Haydn, "String Quartet in C major", but at the time the only title I had ever heard for it was "Deutschland Uber Alles". The little Jewish boy inside me had a moment of panic. That's when I looked more closely at the church bulletin in my hand and saw the author's name. That melody like many by the classic composers had been co-opted by governments and religious organizations alike.

After my heart slowed to a normal rate I again become swept up in the service. The readings from the Old Testament were familiar and the sermon, though I do not remember its subject stirred me. It seems that Rev. Piazza was cut from the same cloth as Rabbi Olan of my youth. His sermon was interesting, intellectually stimulating and filled with questions posed to the congregation. He actually expected his flock to think and more importantly to live out their faith.

At the end of the service, the congregation was called to communion, and though it was an "open communion" accessible to anyone who wished to partake, I sat it out while Patrick went through the sacrament alone. I was still an observer, and it would take a few more weeks before I felt comfortable enough to join him.

The best thing about visiting the Cathedral of Hope, was finding a group of Christians who were very unlike the Christians I had been exposed to in college and my childhood. These people were friendly, open and about as non-judgmental as any I had ever met. After the service, several of the leathermen who attended the Bible study came up and welcomed me. Later we all went out for brunch at a nearby restaurant. The event reminded me of the "trough feedings" that usually followed an AL-Anon or AA meeting. Lots of discussion and fellowship, but at a level of intimacy that was refreshing.

I guess it's not surprising that I felt right at home. These brunches reminded me of the Friday evening dinners following services at the Temple. Though I was a child at the time, I was included in these lively discussions about whatever theological or social issue had been the topic of the sermon. Since both Michael Piazza and Levi Olan both liked to challenge people beliefs and social biases, these discussions could be very lively indeed. After only a few weeks I was beginning to feel right at home.

About three months later I would make a decision that has shaped much of my life since. I asked Jackson and Roger to come over one evening and talk to me about their beliefs as Christians. We had a long and serious discussion and what I found was not quite what I expected.

Both men had slightly different views on what being a Christian meant. They were remarkably candid in their discussion, and I will always value that evening.

I had been reading a lot about Christianity, and the book that influenced me the most was written by a Hindu man. Mohandas Gandhi's writings about Christianity had been assembled into an anthology which I found to be a delightfully readable and candid assessment of the religion. Surprisingly, Gandhi looked on Jesus teachings as some of the finest examples of how to live ever written. He was extremely enthusiastic about the "Sermon on the Mount" and called it one of the greatest theological works ever.

I found that my spiritual ideals and principals fit nicely with those expounded by Jesus, and I sincerely felt that he would have been someone whose example I could happily follow in my daily life. That in combination with my discussion with Jackson and Roger led me to the conclusion that I wanted to take the next step in my faith journey. I made the decision to be baptized and join the church.

Since that day, my faith journey has continued. Though I found a church home at Cathedral of Hope, I had not fully explored what it meant to be Christian, and more to the point what it meant to be a gay, leatherman Christian. That journey is still continuing, and that is what the remainder of this story is about.

A Cross on My Leathers

I wear a small cross on my leather vest. It blends in with all the run pins, friendship pins and club patches, but it still sticks out for some folks. I get a lot of questions about it and that's just fine with me. Any of my friends could tell you that I love having conversations, especially of a spiritual nature. I sometimes think I should have gone into the clergy instead of becoming a writer and filmmaker.

Since a good number of the people I meet are in the leather/BDSM/ fetish community, I get a lot of questions specifically regarding the cross and my being a Christian. Most of them begin with the question, "how can you be a leatherman into SM and still be a Christian?"

Luckily, thanks to a lot of work done by clergy people like Troy Perry, Michael Piazza, Mel White and Nancy Wilson the question of being gay and Christian is usually not part of that inquiry. Within the circle of folks I associate with, that question has already been answered but people still have a lot of trouble wrapping their heads around the leather/BDSM part of the equation.

I suppose a lot of people still feel that SM is about hurting people, and that idea seems pretty un-Christian. It is understandable when one considers the issue strictly on the surface. Almost everyone is familiar with the persecution of Christians by the Romans and conversely alleged heretics by the Christians later in history. What happens is that most people, even many of those who engage in SM still lump what we do in the dungeon and bedroom in with abusive and violent acts.

Before tossing this book in the trash, hear me out. There is a very big difference between abusive acts and SM. Though most people in the scene know this, sometime deep in their subconscious they have doubts. Much the same as many gay men and lesbians, even those who are not closeted, still harbor the seeds of homophobia in their subconscious. It is not always obvious, but it can still pop up when you least expect it.

Consider the phrase that is used in personal ads by gay men seeking partners, "straight-acting". What does that mean? Since I was once guilty of using this term to describe myself, I think I can give a pretty good definition. It means not overtly effeminate or flamboyantly nelly. Why is that a bad thing? Well in itself it is not. I am not attracted to men who are effeminate, but I can say with certainty that I have at least once or twice lapsed into a campy nelly moment. It would also mean that if I was out and about in the company of another man, I probably wouldn't hold hands or act in any way that would draw attention to the fact that I was gay unless it was in a gay-friendly atmosphere.

Now, that said, my natural demeanor does not alert most men's "gaydar", and unless I am dressed in leather or wearing my keys on my belt, you might never know I was anything other than just another middle aged out-of-shape man. That is because of the "tyranny of the norm". This phrase has been used to describe the assumption by the majority of people that everyone is just like them. It's a dangerous and insidious assumption.

Everyone is guilty of it, even gays and lesbians. Consider the last time you saw a celebrity "outed" in the press. If you are anything like me your response would either be "I always figured he or she was," or "I would have never suspected." Either way your blanket assumptions had lumped that individual into a category without knowing the facts.

Most white Christian American's assume everyone who is white is Christian. Now, unless you are an idiot, you know that is not true, but that assumption still persists at a subconscious level. It can still affect the way you treat others and how you react to them. Similarly, most straight people assume everyone is straight. That is why you hear heterosexuality referred to as normal, and any other form of sexual expression as abnormal. The truth is usually much more complex than those simple assumptions and that is where the problem lies.

As I said earlier, I am not prone to public displays of affection, but sometimes I do hold hands with my partner in public and it is a liberating experience. The "tyranny of the norm" creates a double standard that makes it acceptable and "normal" for straight couples to cuddle, hold hands and kiss in public. When a gay or lesbian couple do it we are "flaunting our sexuality."

Inside many of us kinky folks, there is still the assumption that everyone is "normal" (i.e. not kinky). Because of that sometimes we feel like we might be abnormal and that breeds a kind of internalized "kinkaphobia" that makes us feel guilty about how we express our sexuality. In the severe cases it leads to keeping our kink in the closet. That manifests itself in many ways, and many of them, such as seeking anonymous encounters in non-kink friendly environments, can be dangerous. In milder instances, it just makes us feel slightly guilty after a night of kinky pleasures, a "guilt hangover" that comes as a mild depression. The overall result is that many people, who on the surface seem perfectly comfortable with their kink, still are struggling with it deep down inside. They have succumbed to the "tyranny of the norm".

Internalized guilt is what kept many gay and lesbian people from pursuing their faith journey in many Christian churches. Additionally, many Christian churches actively condemn and seek to turn away GLBT people or worse, to "cure" them. The shrill voices of people like the late Jerry Falwell promoted hatred toward gay and lesbian people and often external hatred can be absorbed and become internal hatred. If left to fester in a person who is already unsure of their sexual identity, internal hatred can end in physical consequences. It is not surprising that the suicide rate among gay teens is four time higher than that of heterosexual teens, and though there is only anecdotal proof, I lay the blame at the feet of the loudest voices in the Christian right.

That same internalized guilt, that feeling that you are not "normal" leads a lot of leather/BDSM/fetish folks away from the Christian faith to other spiritual traditions that are less judgmental and more accepting of differences.

Given all this, how can I still be a Christian? That is the real question people are asking, though they might not elaborate quite as much as I do.

I have a simple and yet complex answer. I am a follower of Jesus. More specifically, Jesus, as recorded in the New Testament, says nothing against being gay, lesbian, kinky or anything else having to do with a person's sexuality. He does speak eloquently against infidelity and dishonesty. He talks of living a life that is honest and giving. He preached against bigotry, intolerance and greed. He preached against war and injustice. He preached a doctrine of nonviolence and peace. I see nothing in his teachings that precludes me from following him even though I am kinky and gay. Moreover, there are little known traditions within the Christian church that honor the kinds of experiences I have in the dungeon, and in a good way. Now that is a religion I can truly say I can follow.

Before getting into the Christian kinky closet, I want to go a little further into how I define myself as a Christian. I have done considerable studying of Christianity, its roots and beliefs. I did a lot of this before getting baptized and have continued that study to this very day.

I am often reminded of the quote in John 8:12 when Jesus says, "I am the light of the world: he that follows me shall not walk in the darkness, but shall have the light of life."

Light is not a single color, but it is made up of both the visible and invisible spectrum. I have found Christianity is a religion that presents itself more as a broad spectrum than a single focused beam. Granted, each denomination and sect seems to have its own dogma and focus, yet with the exception of the most rigid orthodoxy, most consider all Christians as "one body in Christ" (Romans 12:5). This allows for a broad spectrum of interpretation of what it means to be a Christian.

For me the most important part of my belief and my religion is not based on a dispensational view of salvation and the end times but rather a practical view of Christ's example and his teachings as guides for living. The concerns for the after-life in heaven or whatever form it might take are not the concerns of this world. In this world, Jesus makes it clear that we have important work to do. The practical steps Christians are asked to take are too numerous to quote them all, but my favorites appear in Mathew 25:35-36. Here Jesus is telling a parable and in it he says this as part of his story, "For I was hungry and you gave me something to eat, I was thirsty and you gave me something to drink, I was a stranger and you invited me in, I needed clothes and you clothed me, I was sick and you looked after me, I was in prison and you came to visit me."

In John 15:12-13 Jesus is quoted, "My command is this: Love each other as I have loved you. Greater love has no one than this, that he lay down his life for his friends."

Those sound like specific action items in my book, and when I read them I find they give me a pretty good direction for my life. With this kind of guidance I find being a follower of Jesus both challenging and fulfilling.

Passages like these also give me an insight into my own kink. When Jesus states in John 13:34, "A new command I give you: Love one another." I understand that to mean pretty much what he says. When I am in the dungeon, playing with a partner, I try to keep this commandment in mind. In other words, I am constantly aware that the person I am playing with is one of God's children just like me. I try to always show them the respect I would expect in any similar situation.

So I suspect you might be questioning how an SM Top can do this and still have fun? It's pretty easy. I remember that any partner with whom I play has given their body into my hands for the scene. Though we have negotiated to whatever degree necessary beforehand, there is an element of trust. As I have said before, that trust is something I find sacred, and especially so when I remember Jesus commandment. My pleasure as an SM Top comes from taking a bottom to a place they could not get by themselves. It is a journey to a peak experience, and whether it is a simple scene or something very elaborate, the goal is the same. The power exchange that happens in an SM scene is a shared experience. The person I play with and I both take a journey through our play and if I guide that journey with love in my heart, I find we both prosper from the experience. When I talk of love, I am not speaking of the same love my boy and I have for one another. That is reserved for that special bond between us and it is a covenant I keep. The love I have for a play partner in an SM scene is that love I have for all God's children. It is born of respect for the individual and a nurturing instinct I think is inherent in all human beings.

How does it work in practice? Well, for example, when I am flogging a partner I use my flogger as an extension of my body. Its tresses caress and bite the skin of the bottom much like my own hands and mouth might, but in a way that is intended to produce an intense sensation. The pain caused through an SM flogging is more than just pain, it can be an erotic experience or just a cathartic release. Much like a very intense massage can release pent up tensions and emotions, the same is true for a flogging.

We SM players are "differently pleasured" and because of that something many folks would find intolerable is just invigorating for us. Because of this, I know that my actions as a Top are in some way pleasurable, cathartic or invigorating for the bottom, and because of that

I can release any guilt I might have felt and concentrate on producing the best experience possible for both of us. That is what SM with love is about.

I am constantly annoyed when I hear Tops or Doms speak about "playing" someone. To my way of thinking it objectifies that person and makes them less than human. Tops do not "play" people like CDs; they play "with" people. That distinction makes all the difference in both the Tops experience and the way he or she treats the bottom or sub. I have watched many scenes at a dungeon party where the Top or Dom seems to be just going through the motions. They have sufficient skills, but they never seem to connect with the person they are playing with at anything more than a superficial level. What a waste of energy for the Top! I have to believe that if they really tried to connect with their bottom or sub through the act or their play, both participants would have a better experience.

I suspect many Tops have never had that deep power exchange that comes from a scene that is entered into as a loving act. The best Tops and Doms I have ever met and watched immerse themselves in the scene no matter who they play with. They use their talents and skills for an enriching experience for both themselves and their partners. The power exchange is so profound even those watching are affected. I take that as further proof of the love expressed in an SM scene.

Each time I play in the dungeon just as every day of my life I attempt to live out Jesus' words from Mathew 22:39, "Love your neighbor as yourself."

Disciples in Leather

The leathermen who I met when I first came out into the leather/BDSM scene didn't seem to worry much about the spiritual relevance of their activities. They just lived out their kink as honestly and openly as they could. Things were different then and being out as a gay man was hard enough, being out as a leatherman would have been unthinkable except for a lucky few whose jobs and lives made it possible.

Most of us lived a dual existence. We wore the trappings of the vanilla world during the day and leather at night. It was that duality that gave some of what we did its excitement. We were part of a secret underworld society. There was something illicit and vaguely sinister about being into leather/BDSM back then. That is part of what made it so attractive, just as movie villains are often the most sexually charged characters, so too were leathermen. We were the "bad boys" of the gay subculture, and because of that there was often an aura of danger and mystery that surrounded us. And, we liked it!

That "outlaw" quality set us apart from the mainstream of both the gay and the straight world. Yes it was true that we liked our sexual pleasures rougher than most, but in reality there were no more dangerous people in the leather community than in any other segment of the population. The whole leather image did have a down side as well. It meant that leathermen were often excluded when it came to political activism and public events. To a lot of gay and lesbian activists, leathermen and leatherwomen were negative stereotypes that should be excluded to avoid controversy and bad press.

Like drag queens and cross-dressers, leathermen were looked upon as not politically correct. Never mind that the drag queens and leatherfolk helped motivate and instigate the whole gay power movement! As both outlaws and outcasts, we have often not had a place at the table when it came to many movements that affected our lives. There is a curious similarity between our tribe of outcasts and the motley group who followed Jesus. He surrounded himself with the marginalized and politically incorrect. He told parables about adulterous women and Samaritans, and hung out with tax collectors and other marginal folks. These people were very strange types to be in the company of a Jew.

When I think about Jesus extended family, his disciples, I am reminded of my own group of close friends. These are people who chose to be in each other's company, not because of blood relations but because of a commonality of interests. The disciples were chosen by Jesus, or were drawn to him by his spirit and teachings. The leather family I am part of was drawn together by a spirit as well. I won't press the metaphor too much more, because there are significant differences, but not surprisingly, many of the leatherfolk who are part of our group are spiritual seekers, much like the disciples.

I think after the AIDS crisis of the1980's decimated so much of the gay and leather community in particular, we who were left began to look deeper into our own lives. Personally, I saw so many of my friends die that I spent a lot of time considering my own mortality and the whole "meaning of life" thing. I found I wasn't alone in this. There was a bit of a spiritual revival in the late 1980's that is directly related to the AIDS epidemic. Just as gay activism was energized with an urgency that it never had before, a lot of gay and lesbian people turned to religions and spiritual groups in record numbers.

We also looked at our behaviors and found that we couldn't do all of the things we did sexually anymore without putting ourselves and our partners at risk. We found that much of what we still did was very safe from an epidemiological standpoint. Leathermen could still have a night of rough play, including floggings, spankings, bondage and electrical play with minimal or no danger of transmission of diseases. Amazingly, because of our esoteric pleasures, a good deal of our play was actually safer than the "vanilla" sex games mainstream gays and lesbians played.

For me this realization had a profound effect. Though I could not engage in unprotected sex any more, I could still spend a night in a dungeon and find much the same satisfaction. It was as though I had discovered a gift I never knew I had, and other people discovered it, too.

Through local organizations like the National Leather Association – Dallas and men's play clubs, like the Disciple of De Sade, the word got out that there was a lot more than vanilla sex out there. People who had never considered anything but "normal" gay and lesbian sex began opening their minds to the kinky pleasures that leather/BDSM offered. A series of Thursday night seminars was held in cooperation with the Dallas County Health Department and the Disciples of De Sade, called itself "Beyond Vanilla". The popularity of these meetings led to what has become a nationally known event held annually here in Dallas of the same name.

People were drawn to the leather/BDSM scene as they searched for ways to keep their sex lives safe and still maintain the excitement. Leather was beginning to be seen as a viable alternative to "normal" sex! Many leatherfolk, myself included, found ourselves becoming more and more involved in education. We were spreading the good news about what we did in the dungeon and the bedroom. About that time a curious thing also happened, heterosexual people began showing up at the seminars as well. Now there had been kinky straight people for as long as kink had been around, but they rarely mixed with the gay and lesbian community. Now here they were actively seeking to share our knowledge and share theirs with us.

Now before my straight friends string me up by my thumbs, I have to say there had been heterosexual kink groups around our area for a long time. They were mostly underground groups with coded names like "People Exchanging Power" and "The Chili Pepper Appreciation Society". The difference was that the gay and lesbian groups actively pursued educating the community on a scale no other groups had done before. Some of this was out of the sense of urgency brought on by the epidemic. The result of this educational move was a dissemination of information about safe play that continues to this day.

A curious side effect of this effort was the inclusion of the spiritual side of BDSM. I think that because we had been forced to really analyze what we were doing in our play we began to see the possibilities of deeper meaning in it. Sometimes a crisis can focus your attention on details that you might have missed before. Finding that much of what we were already doing was already safer sex made me consider the possibility that we had been given a gift. It is a gift that we have shared with others and in some small way it is enriching the loves of the people who receive it. If that's not a spiritual side effect, I don't know what is.

Still, many in our community feel that they are still outcasts or outsiders when it comes to spiritual matters. They have given up on mainstream religions in many cases without even really trying to understand them. It is to those leatherfolk that I try to bring the message spoken by Jesus so many years ago. It is that message that spoke to me when I was pursuing my spiritual quest. I am still pursuing that quest and I suspect I always will be. Luckily, the words of Jesus still resonate with me, and I have found they bring comfort and enlightenment to many leatherfolk as well, if they take the time to listen to them.

That's the problem for some people, both leatherfolk and "vanilla" alike. We spend much of our days talking and working and bustling so fast that we rarely take time to read or listen or meditate or pray. It is amazing the profound effect just slowing down for a few moments in the day can have on your life. For me, it gives me a chance to reflect and try to understand not only my inner thoughts, but to listen for the voice of God. No I don't hear voices, but I do hear God speak. I hear God through the words of Jesus. I hear God through the voices of others, my friends and associates. I hear God in a sermon or song at church. I hear God sometimes in my own thoughts. But I would not hear anything if I didn't actively make time to listen.

There is a line in the 46th Psalm that reads, "Be still, and know that I am God." I find that is pretty good advice for my life. The act of "being still" is the listening I mentioned earlier. It is in these times of stillness that insight often comes to me. The wonderful comedienne Gracie Allen once said, "Never put a period where God put a comma." I believe she was talking about listening for God's voice.

What this all comes down to is my belief that the words of God are not captive to the pages of a bible, nor are they the property of any one religion or sect. My church, which is now affiliated with the United Church of Christ, uses a slogan "God is still speaking" in its promotional material. That really resonates with me, otherwise I would be left to try to decipher the message from God set down so long ago in words that have been translated and sometimes mistranslated over the centuries. I do believe God's word is in the bible, but I also believe it is to be found in much more contemporary sources like those of Gracie Allen.

This is at the heart of why I became a Christian. I found a church and community that actively sought God's guidance and worked to follow it in the world today. Now, how God's word resonates for my leather life might seem odd, but I find it is a vital part of my spiritual growth.

Listening for Leather in God's Words

When I first joined the church, I became involved with a discussion group called "Shouts in the Wilderness". The group took this name because one of the only characters in the New Testament who is described as wearing leather is John the Baptist. (Mark 1:6 – "And John was clothed with camel's hair, and had a leathern girdle about his loins…") John was what we might call today a "modern primitive". He lived off the land eating locusts and honey and performed spiritual rituals in the outdoors rather than in the Temple.

That group was instrumental in my spiritual development and I eventually became the leader of it and still work with it today. We discuss spiritual and biblical topics as well as leather related topics. It is amazing how often the two subjects blend, and it is because of that experience that I began searching the scriptures for specific stories and references that could be interpreted through a leather reading. I believe theological folks call this scriptural hermeneutics and as I understand it, it means to mine the scripture for deeper meanings. Without the theological baggage, our group does just that.

I have read the Bible in a couple of different translations and found a variety of other ancient books that were considered sacred writings in the Jewish and Christian faiths. The "Gospel of Thomas" is one of my favorites. This "lost book" of the New Testament was unearthed in the excavations at Nag Hammadi, Egypt in 1945. It was one of the scriptures tossed out during the canonization of the Bible back in the early days of the church. It reads much more like a book of eastern philosophy and basically is not a story but a list of sayings of Jesus. This book among others has been the subject of discussion for our group.

It was through this study that I really became comfortable with wearing that cross on my leathers I spoke about earlier. I still find gathering with this close circle of friends is invigorating and enlightening, and sometimes for the most surprising reasons.

One of our members was browsing through a commentary on the Old Testament and a chapter caught his eye. The book, *Queer Commentary on the Hebrew Bible*, (Ken Stone, Editor) had an essay by Lori Rowlett on the story of Samson & Delilah. She interprets it through the queer lens as a story of a butch bottom and an SM femme Top. It sparked a lot of discussion and not surprisingly a group of leathermen saw this story as a tale of a male sub and a Femme Domme. Samson, the pushy bottom, keeps teasing Delilah to tie him up tighter and with very specific bonds in each of their play sessions. Samson apparently does not know Delilah has other less benign plans. Still, it was an interesting experience listening to my friends becoming animated in their discussions of a story that most of us had forgotten long ago.

Seeing the faces of leathermen light up while discussing the Bible was something I had never experienced. Each person saw something different in the text, and though we all understood the point of the story, we find that the details were presented in a way that gave a hint to something more. The storyteller understood the flirtatious banter between Samson and Delilah and his teasing her with various details of the bondage that would truly hold him as her prisoner had to be more than just a clever plot line. Samson tells Delilah how to bind him. "If anyone ties me with seven fresh thongs that have not been dried, I'll become as weak as any other man." Of course he breaks them easily and the whole scene is repeated the next night with different requests from Samson. If that does not sound like a pushy bottom I don't know what does, and that's exactly the impression the group got as well. We found the flirtation with the danger that was Delilah as a kind of edge-play for Samson. He knows he is risking his freedom and perhaps his life, but that is part of the thrill. His game goes so far as to actually get him into trouble when he reveals the real secret of his strength and is enslaved and blinded by the Philistines.

Applying this same technique, we explored lots of other texts and found characters that in our reading became easy to identify with. As I mentioned in an earlier chapter, the story of Jesus and the Centurion from Mathew contained another character our group saw with a leather sensibility.

In the story a centurion comes to Jesus and tells Jesus that his servant or slave is paralyzed and sick. Jesus offers to go to him, but the centurion says he need only "say the word" and his servant will be healed. The centurion shows a great faith in the power of Jesus and God's word. What he also shows is a love for his servant or slave. Slaves were property, but one would hardly expect a commander to go out of his way to find a spiritual healer to cure him from sickness. The act of seeking out Jesus and requesting his help reminded many in our group of the lengths to which they would go to for one of their partners. Even the leathermen who had "boys" and "slaves" said the depth of their love would move them to go to any length to find help. A discussion of the obligations of a Master to his slaves and a Daddy to his boys sprang from the biblical story.

Another lively discussion came by sheer coincidence. A few days before the meeting a group of protestors had picketed our church. These people, claiming to be doing God's work, were evicted from our property several times and finally were warned by the police to stay outside the church property. They huddled on the street corner across from the church parking lot and made a big production of "praying for our sins".

That Sunday evening at our discussion group we had already announced we would be studying Mathew 6, the chapter containing the Lord's Prayer as well as this admonishment from Jesus, "And when you pray, do not be like the hypocrites, for they love to pray standing in the synagogues and on the street corners to be seen by men. I tell you the truth, they have received their reward in full." The irony was not lost on our group.

Our group expanded the discussions to include interesting aspects of Christian history. Particularly interesting were the early Christian Ascetics who used the disciplines of fasting and isolation as a way to purify their minds and prepare for the gift of enlightenment. Not surprisingly, a few members of our group found similarities in the ascetic practices and sensory deprivation as practiced in a leather context. In a very limited sense, an experience bound in the wrappings of "mummification" is a temporary ascetic practice. For those unfamiliar with "mummification" as practiced in the BDSM world, it involved a person being wrapped from head to toe in some kind of material that restricts all movement and deprives the person being wrapped on both freedom of movement but because of the wrapping the sense of touch is dulled.

The actual practice of mummification takes into account safety of the person encased, with adequate openings for clear breathing and a wrapping that is tight, but not so much as to cut off circulation or inhibit respiration. Materials used can be plastic wrap, plastic wrap layered with duct tape, cloth or even rubber strips. The effect is similar no matter which material is used.

People who are mummified often speak of out-of-body experiences and often a profound peacefulness. Some even call the experience spiritual, and that was the connection our group picked up on.

Other Christian ascetics in the first few centuries of the faith used much more extreme forms of physical mortification as either repentance or as a way of rejecting the fear of death. Syrian ascetics would even suspend themselves with ropes so as to remain upright and not lie down. It doesn't take a biblical scholar to see some interesting parallels between these practices and the exotic bondage arrangements we perform in the dungeon or playspace. Our group realized that we shared many common experiences with the ancient Christians, and though ours were done for entirely different reasons, the effects were recognizably similar.

In fact many of the practices of early Christian holy men are among the same things we do in the dungeon today. Had we been born a couple of thousand years ago, we might have been monks or priests. It is no accident that ascetics in all societies are often looked upon as sacred people or holy men. From the shamans of Native American religious practices to the Sufi Fakirs and Christian flagellants, religions have recognized the power of physical pain in transcending the mortal world and entering the realm of the spirit. The tradition cuts across almost every religious tradition.

Having had some of those experiences, I can tell you they often make me want to repeat them. I can understand fully how an ascetic holy man cold spend many of his days engaged in these practices. I discussed this phenomenon in my book, *Playing with Pain*. In that book I explain what I call the pain/pleasure continuum. There are few clear cut lines between pain and pleasure, and in recent medical research it looks like the same centers in the brain are stimulated by both sensations. This really blurs the line between pain and pleasure, and it is in this gray area that the leatherfolk play.

SM experiences, if they are satisfying, often leave the participants wanting to repeat them. No surprise there. The surprise to non-leather people is that the pain experienced in a scene can be something that is actually desired. It is that pain that "hurts so good". For example, a person who has gotten a tattoo may want more tattoos. They may desire them because they like the way they look, an aesthetic appeal to create a living artwork from their body, or they may seek the experience of being tattooed. That desire comes from the physical processes that kick in when the tattoo artist begins his or her work. The chemistry of the body as the needles enter the skin produces a reaction from the brain and that sets all sorts of natural opiates rushing through the bloodstream. The "runner's high" that is often mentioned by long distance runners is the same thing, but in the case of the person who wants the tattoo, it's part of the goal, rather than just a side effect.

I suspect much of the reward for the ascetic is that same natural "high", though in the case of holy men and shamans it is interpreted as achieving a spiritual state. I tend to believe it is in actuality both. I feel that when we enter ecstatic states such as those produced by ascetic practices or SM play, we become not only aroused, but are put into an altered state of consciousness. Though the physical processes can be explained away by a science, there remains a tangible heightened awareness that defies a simple explanation. It is that state that often results in a feeling of spiritual connectedness between play partners and in some ways between all leatherfolk and BDSM practitioners. There is a commonality of experience that forms a communion for leathermen and women. It is almost a sacramental rite when it is sufficiently profound.

I used to hear leathermen talk about a rite of passage into the leather community. What they were talking about was having that first "peak experience" where as either a Top or a bottom, you "got it". It was an experience that opened your eyes to the possibilities of a scene being more than just foreplay. It was the moment you found yourself feeling connected with your play partner in so deep a way that for the moment time stood still, and whatever was happening around you became just background noise to the deep experience of which you were a part.

Beyond the physical/spiritual connection I feel with those early Christian ascetics which I will discuss later, I find a practical and ethical system for living in the teachings of Jesus that gives me a guide to living. It is that path to living a productive and fulfilling life that really centers my life and my spirituality. I found this path both through looking at the scriptures in a conventional sense as well as filtered though a leather sensibility. It is the voice of Jesus that calls to the deepest part of my soul and speaks to my place in the realm of human existence as well as the realm of God.

Setting My Boots on a Path to the Cross

I suspect many people who read this will promptly ask that question I was peppered with during my brief time at Baylor University, "do I accept Jesus Christ as my own personal Lord and savior?" Well, the answer to that one is a whole lot more involved than a simple "yes" or "no". I think the answer to that question cannot be given in such a flip manner, because it is one of the most profound ones in the entire Christian religion, and in my opinion, not a litmus test for believers.

Much of what I learned of Christianity prior to my actually becoming a Christian had to do with matters of salvation and the afterlife. That brings to mind a scenario from Dante's Devine Comedy with his poetic images of heaven, purgatory and hell. I personally think a lot of people have confused Dante's vision with the Bible and religious teachings. It is not a religious text, it is allegorical poetry and political commentary, but I will leave any analysis of the great poet to a scholar. I love Dante, and I grew up reading his epic poem and often became lost in the illustrations of Gustav Dore that adorned the book in my father's library. Those illustrations, specifically those of hell, became the basis of a lot of my early sexual fantasies. As a budding leatherman, it is no surprise that pictures of naked sinners, specifically muscular naked men being tortured and whipped was somehow erotic. That, however, is not the basis of my spiritual and religious beliefs.

I am not a big believer in the Dante version of heaven and hell. Though it makes for great poetry it makes for really bad theology. Putting all of creation into a dichotomy ruled by either a sadistic fallen angel or an egotistical patriarchal creator does not work for me. The never ending battle of good and evil that forms the basis of some religious dogma seems like pretty shaky ground for a foundation of a modern religion. If I believed God is the vengeful despot often imaged in the Old Testament, then I would probably still be a Jew. If I believed God is the commander of an army who must battle the forces of evil in the book of Revelation, then I don't find Christianity very appealing either. I have to suspect that is the basis of many people's crisis of faith, both in the vanilla world and in the leather community.

Those images of God are what I refer to as the "Little Golden Book of Bible Stories" theology. They might work well for teaching kids a few moral lessons, but in the end they use the threat of damnation as motivation. Quite frankly, even if there were a hell for sinners, most people are far too short sighted for that threat to work for long. If people really did base every action on their lives on planning for a future that will last "forever" then we would all have big fat savings accounts and there would be no wars or global conflicts.

It seems to me that any theology that is based on fear of punishment at the hands of an all powerful God only leads to a crisis of faith when that punishment fails to materialize for people who obviously disobey God's rules. It also gets pretty hard to swallow when you lead what you feel is a saintly life only to find yourself in a horrible accident or deprived of the basic necessities of living. I know of many folks who have found themselves in really awful circumstances and become despondent wondering what they had done to deserve their fate.

It is also thin theological ice to believe that salvation can be achieved by using a magic formula. Some people believe that saying they "take Jesus to be a personal Lord and savior" is all that is needed to excluding themselves from a fiery pit for eternity. Sounds more like a secret handshake for a fraternity than a spiritual belief system. What kind of message does that sort of a theology send? Go ahead and sin, lie, cheat and steal, as long as you say the magic words, "I take Jesus as my personal savior" you get into heaven. I have a hard time believing that God passes out *Get out of Jail Free* cards.

So if my version of Christianity is not about going to heaven when I die, what is it about?

Well I believe in salvation, but it is not the kind of salvation that rescues your soul from the fiery pit of hell. I believe Jesus brought a very real and practical guide to salvation from the hell that many people create here on earth. In my theology, it doesn't take a fallen angel to make people miserable. I don't think even Satan could do as good a job of spreading suffering and pestilence as we human beings do. Everyday folks like me and you manage to create enough opportunities for bad things to happen. Occasionally, a real doozie comes along like a Stalin or Hitler who really spreads the misery around in mind boggling ways, but the point is if we listen to Jesus teachings and actually try to follow them we can be saved from a good deal of misery.

In the Gospel of John, there is a much used passage, "I tell you the truth, no one can see the kingdom of God unless he is born again". Interesting metaphor, "born again" and it could have numerous meanings, but Jesus clarifies it with the following, "I tell you the truth, no one can enter the kingdom of God unless he is born of water and the Spirit."

What I find in this passage is an obvious reference to baptism. Baptism is an act that symbolically washes away the past sins. It gives people a clean slate to start fresh, freed from the baggage of the guilt and shame of their past mistakes. With your mind clear of the regret and roadblocks you can get a clearer vision of what Jesus means by the "Kingdom of God". Again, I am not interpreting that as meaning a cloudy place full of flying angels, instead I hear Jesus telling his disciples in Mathew "I will give you the keys of the kingdom of heaven; whatever you bind on earth will be bound in heaven, and whatever you loose on earth will be loosed in heaven." To me Jesus is clearly speaking of earthly actions being very important, in fact the keys he gives can bring about God's heaven on earth.

I look further in the text and find specific instructions on how to do what Jesus asks. "If anyone would come after me, he must deny himself and take up his cross and follow me. For whoever wants to save his life will lose it, but whoever loses his life for me will find it." That is about as clear a call to action as I can find. Taking up the cross means taking on the burden of doing God's work, following Jesus and finding a new life by leaving the old life behind. Maybe that is what being born again is all about? I think so, because when I do follow Jesus example I find myself and my world a happier place.

If you haven't figured it out by now, I am not a fundamentalist. I cannot read the Bible and believe that every word should be taken literally; if I did I would have been arrested long ago for killing disobedient children and stoning people who eat shellfish as enumerated in the laws of the Old Testament.

I believe the Bible is a collection of books that in many ways tells the story of people's encounter with the divine. Each story is grasping at explaining the unexplainable and in doing so they all fall a little short. I am reminded of the ancient Chinese philosopher Lao Tzu who says, "The Tao that can be described is not the eternal Tao". I think the same is true for my concept of God. If I can describe God in words, I am not describing God. It makes reading the scriptures less intimidating and also fascinating as I discover the many ways believers have attempted to put into words the indescribable.

I read the Bible with the eyes of not only a gay leatherman, but of a 21st century human being. We are creatures of our times, and trying to superimpose ancient texts on modern life can lead to big problems. Rather we must find in the scriptures relevant truths that still speak to us. It is "cherry picking" to an extent, but that same "cherry picking" goes on with fundamentalists as well. In honesty, we find what we want to find in scriptures. I only hope that what I find will lead to something better for everyone I interact with and lessen the overall suffering in the world. It is in that way that we really bring about the Kingdom of Heaven.

So why Jesus? Lots of other religions have good paths for living a virtuous life, what is it about Christianity that I find appealing? I think part of that answer is pretty direct. Because of my background, my cultural history and my personal philosophy, Jesus makes the most sense for me. I dearly love the writings of Lao Tzu, the ideals of the Buddha, readings from the blessed Koran, the ancient stories of the Hindu gods and goddesses, but the Bible and its words resonate with me more.

I believe that there are many paths to God's realm, a belief that was even alluded to by Jesus but His story is the one I choose to follow. It fits well with the Western culture, and incorporates what I learned as a child raised as a Jew. Jesus was a Jew, so it's not a big jump to find myself following in his path.

Jesus was also a non-violent rabble rouser. He caused trouble by speaking truth to power. He didn't like the status quo and because he took steps to change it he was arrested and eventually executed. I like rabble rousers and I always have. People who see the status quo as unjust, biased and oppressive and who do things to make a difference and bring about justice and peace are my kind of people. Activists who take on great social ills such as equal rights, freedom of expression and peace are often persecuted and in some cases they are arrested and executed. The admirable thing about them is they have a willingness to put their beliefs to work. Jesus put his beliefs to work!

Growing up in the 1960's and 1970's I participated in protests over the Vietnam War, marches for civil rights and organizing in the Gay Rights movement. I was young, but I knew that if things were ever going to change it would take people working to make it so. Jesus lived his life in that way. He preached peace where the authorities pursued war. Jesus preached of God's inclusive grace, where the clergy of the time set barriers to faith. Jesus was politically incorrect in the Roman world, and for me that's the kind of person I would follow had I been there. Now, I follow

Jesus spirit and his teachings. Luckily some folks wrote down much of what he said, and though it has been scrambled and often mistranslated for ulterior motives, much of Jesus words still remain.

The other factor that guided me toward Jesus was finding a church home. When I found the Cathedral of Hope, a place where I could comfortably join others in the worship of God and be exactly who I am with no masks or pretensions, I knew I had found something special. When I attend a service, sitting with many of my leather brothers and sisters, wearing our leathers and club colors, I feel comfortable and at home. The other members of the congregation feel at home as well. We have transgendered members, flamboyant gay men, butch lesbians, straight singles and couples and even a few poly-amorous family groups. We are a very different kind of congregation, and for that I am very grateful. Our church doctrine of God's extravagate grace is palpable in that building.

We are a congregation that occasionally has differences, but none so great that we cannot settle them by working together. Under the guidance of our Senior Pastor Dr. Jo Hudson, we have affiliated ourselves with the United Church of Christ, and though many people confuse this with the Church of Christ, it is a very progressive denomination. UCC sprang from the merging of the Congregationalist Church, one of our country's oldest denominations, and the Evangelical and Reformed Church in 1957. As part of that denomination, we are continuing our service and outreach work to not only the GLBT community, but the greater Dallas community. Additionally our services are broadcast in many cities on public access TV and over the internet worldwide.

Part of my attraction to the Cathedral of Hope is the kind of hands-on service to the community we are involved in. During the years I have been part of COH, I participated in many service projects and ministries. One of the most profound experiences I have had with COH was participating for several years in the "People Helping People" project.

In cooperation with the City of Dallas our church gathered teams of people to work over a weekend to remodel and renovate the homes of low-income homeowners whose houses were in violation of the city building codes. Some of these homes only required being scraped and repainted, while others needed major construction and repairs. I have done both and twice lead a team of workers during these projects.

The most rewarding experience took place when our group, "Shouts in the Wilderness" and other volunteers from the church worked on a home owned by a very frail African American woman in the southern part of the city. The neighborhood was badly deteriorated and her house needed many repairs to bring it to code, additionally she needed a new railing on her porch and better steps to make it easier for her when she went out.

We arrived early on a Saturday and worked until dark. A team of 16 people including my boy and my friends completely scraped her house and repainted it, rebuilt her screens, added new steps and a new door on her porch and cleared trash from the property. We came back late Sunday to finish up and clean away the construction mess. She invited us in and gave us sweet tea and some cookies she had baked. Her whole family came over and celebrated the work and thanked us. Additionally people in the neighborhood saw lots of cars and trucks with rainbow and leather flags. As we drove away, we were greeted with friendly waves and occasional cheers from people on the street.

That was nice but the real reward was seeing her house looking better than it had in years. Like a ripple on a pond that house might inspire others to do similar work and with it the whole neighborhood and the city will become a better place.

That is just one example of the kind of work our church does in Jesus name. We hold free health fairs for the neighborhood, provide school supplies for hundreds of poor children at local schools, feed hundreds of families at Thanksgiving and Christmas time and much more. Our church also feed the hungry souls of thousands of people who have been turned away from other places. That is the kind of church and community I find hard to resist.

Living Out of the Box

It seems that every day there is another politician caught with his pants down. I mean that literally. The news stories of public officials being busted by police for soliciting sex in places like men's rooms have become commonplace. Funny how it always seems to be a conservative politician who is caught, too?

I think that kind of behavior comes from trying to keep all the different aspects of a person's personality isolated and distinct from other traits and areas. I do not have any psychological research to back this up, but I have personal experience. And no, I have not been caught having public sex!

I tried for many years to keep the different facets of my life neatly separated in little boxes. Like a lot of people, I thought my sexuality and my politics had nothing to do with one another. I was sure that my family life and my politics would never be in conflict. I was equally certain that my spirituality and my kink would never cross paths. Everything was neatly defined and in its appointed place in my life, at least that was the illusion I lived in.

I suspect a lot of people do the same thing and for some it can be successful for a long time, but for me that was not to be. Once I got involved in politics, I found my sexuality was very much an issue. In fact it was through the Dallas Gay Political Caucus (now the Dallas Gay and Lesbian Alliance) that I found my sexuality was in itself a political hot potato. Accepting myself as a gay man was a political act, and in the 1970's it was tantamount to a revolutionary act. So much for those boxes!

Later when I came into leather I found that I was once again bucking the status quo. Funny how I always find myself in that position? As I stated earlier, many in the gay community saw leather as a "PR problem" not a valid expression of radical sexuality. Because of this that pesky political box spilled into my kink box.

I had come out to my family, but that was as a gay man. When I told my mother about the kinky aspects of my life, the family box split wide open. Surprisingly she had fewer problems with the leather than my being gay. Though she had gotten over the shock of my coming out and even joined the nascent PFLAG (Parents and Friends of Lesbians and Gays) it took a while, so I was expecting the same with leather. She fooled me, and told me that she had no problem with me wanting to, "spice up my sex life a little". That was a bit disturbing for me. I didn't want to think of my mother as that open minded.

Then there was that experience in the dungeon. I had a scene where I felt I connected on such a deep level with the person I was playing with I began to look on it as a spiritual moment. Now the spirituality box was getting leaky as well. I had to find a way to make peace with all the different facets of my personality and my sexuality, and that is about the time I heard a sermon that spoke of living an "abundant life".

The particular passage was from John, (10:10) "I came that they may have life, and have it abundantly." In another translation of the Bible the phrase is this, "I have come so they can have life. I want them to have it in the fullest possible way."

That's when I asked myself the question, "how can I have a full and abundant life, if I have not reconciled myself." Living life in discrete segmentation was a recipe for unhappiness and confusion. I had to find a way to embrace all the different areas of my life into one healthy and whole person if I expected to live that "abundant life" Jesus talked about.

What that meant was having a long and honest look at my life from all angles and trying to become comfortable inside my own skin. It meant that my politics, my family, my spirituality and my sexuality would forever be incorporated into one big box. I could no longer label my kink as just something I did once and a while. I could no longer try to separate my spirituality from my sexuality. I could never again hide who I was from my family and friends. It meant being "out" in all aspects of my life.

It was not going to be an easy task, and I suspect Jesus intended it that way when he spoke of it. Identifying as a follower of Jesus was difficult and dangerous during His time and identifying as a gay, kinky Christian was going to be a tall order today. Just as people got angry with Jesus followers back in biblical times, they sometimes get angry with me today, but the gift I receive by living as a fully out person makes up for any difficulty.

Surprisingly, once I tried living my life as a fully out and whole person things got a little easier for me. Not surprisingly, things got more difficult for my friends and associates. My business associates had known me by my occupation as a filmmaker and director. That was easy for them and it let them put me into a little box of their own. A few knew me as a gay man as well, and since I was moving in the advertising and creative circles, that was not too difficult for them to understand as well. They had a box for "gay director".

Once I produced my first short film on the subject of BDSM titled *Leather* in 1995 things got difficult for them. They could deal with the gay part but the kink made them uncomfortable. You see they had some pretty rigid notions of what kinky people were like: dangerous fringe dwellers, a subculture of sick individuals. I didn't fit into that box, and that caused them to have to do some rethinking. Stereotypes die hard, and for some people wrapping their arms around that aspect of my personality was too much. I lost a few associates but thankfully, no close friends.

Add to this mix my new found conversion to Christianity and things got really interesting. This time it was people in the BDSM and leather community who had trouble. They didn't know how to react to someone who called themselves Christian but was honest and open about their kink. It got difficult for them to fit me into the box they labeled as Christian. Lucky for me, I lost no friends in the leather community once they had a chance to talk to me about it. It became a ministry opportunity for me, and before you roll your eyes and imagine me "witnessing the heathens" let me explain. I simply answered their questions as best as I cold regarding my religious and spiritual beliefs. I never try to convert or proselytize anyone. I respect everyone's right to hold whatever beliefs they wish. Mine are important to me just as theirs are important to them.

The great thing about coming out as Christian to my BDSM and leather friends is the conversations it starts. We get to connect on a deeper level when we share our beliefs and that intimacy bonds our friendships even stronger. A side effect has been the friends who ask me to take them to our church. They are genuinely interested in what kind of place it is that openly welcomes leatherfolk as well as GLBT people.

Several of my friends have even become members of the church, without any encouragement from me. That is gratifying because it means that by being open and honest with them about my spirituality and religious beliefs, they found a place they could explore their faith as well.

The people who have the most trouble with my being out as a gay, Christian leatherman are those with the most to lose. I have encountered quite a few people who I could consider fundamentalists. They barely understand anything I say. Their belief system is so rigid that it cannot allow for the possibility of a gay Christian, much less a kinky one. For them anything having to do with sexuality is a one way ticket to hell and damnation. I do not expect them to accept me as "one in Christ" but I am glad I have made their lives a little more uncomfortable. Perhaps that discomfort may someday lead them to an honest examination of their faith and beliefs. I won't hold my breath.

One memorable encounter was with an anti-gay crusader. This man actively sought to confront gay and lesbian people and to "lead them out" of their sinful "life choice". Unfortunately, he chose to do it at our church.

I recognized him from newspaper photos and when I saw him walk into the sanctuary one Sunday morning, I moved to sit beside him. I saw a lesbian friend of mine who realized who he was and did the same thing on the other side. We had him safely pinned between us should he start anything during the service as he had a history of doing in other places. Lucky for us he decided to soft pedal it this particular Sunday, but he did speak to me after the service at an information table Shouts in the Wilderness had set up that day.

I could tell he was confused by the appearance of a group of leathermen in the midst of a church fellowship hall, and he tentatively took one of the brochures we had created telling about our group.

His voice dripped with sarcasm as he read the pamphlet, "Leather huh?"

I smiled and replied, "Just like John the Baptist wore as he was shouting in the wilderness."

He paused with a puzzled look on his face.

"I hope you enjoyed the sermon, Reverend." I said, offering him a licorice whip.

He took it and moved off and was soon to be escorted from the premises. Since he had disrupted the services in the past there was a restraining order on him. I was kind of sad to see him go though. I would never have tried to convince him of anything, I would have just enjoyed getting a better understanding of why he felt it so necessary to block the way that John the Baptist sought to clear so long ago.

I suspect that people like the fundamentalist Reverend might have trouble leading that abundant life Jesus called us to. They are too busy checking their rule books, making judgments and juggling boxes of their own. I have tried to give that up. I have found that by following Jesus and living out and open in all aspects of my life, I find more time to do the work Jesus commanded. Heal the sick; feed the hungry and work to bring peace and justice to the world. Sounds like a tall order but the makings of a full and abundant life to me.

A Few More Words

My life seems to have been a series of "coming out" moments. The first in my memory was when I came out as an adult, my Bar Mitzvah, a rite of passage. The next was my coming out as gay, when I embraced my sexuality. Then there was the first tentative coming out into leather, that first time I walked into a leather bar. I felt like I was coming out all over again when I was baptized and confirmed as a member of my church as a Christian. I suspect there will be more in my future.

It is my sincere hope that others will experience their own spiritual coming out. It is an overwhelmingly positive journey wherever it leads. More importantly, I encourage each person to share that story with their friends. Without that knowledge, others might never know the transformation and freedom that is possible.

The great thing about coming out is that it's kind of like being reborn. By embracing my full self and leaving all the boxes that partitioned my personality behind I become a new person. I still carry the lives and memories of all those people who made me who I am both in the present and past, friends and family. They are that great cloud of witnesses that surround me and their words and actions still guide me in my journey. They have helped clear my path. I get a new perspective on the world and my place in it and sometimes it feels like I can almost see the kingdom of God. With a lot of work and a little luck that vision might become clearer than ever.

Appendix I
Welcome to the World of Leather/Fetish/BDSM

For someone who has no knowledge of the leather community or BDSM I think an introduction might be in order. The acronym, BDSM is short hand for a variety of activities. Bondage, discipline, sadomasochism, would be the most obvious and common usage, but in the alphabet soup of or community the DS part of the equation can stand for dominance and submission and the SM when reversed can stand for master and slave. I have even heard the BD reversed for daddy and boy, the roles assumed by many people both heterosexual and homosexual in our community.

Overwhelming? It was for me when I first was exposed to it all. I had to simplify things to get a handle on it. I did this by considering the reality of what we do. In almost all leather/fetish/BDSM activities, the participants assume roles. The role can be of the severe Master or the obedient slave, the strict but loving Daddy and the sometimes rowdy boy or simply the imperious Domme and the obsequious submissive. What was important for me to remember was that these were roles played out in the bedroom, dungeon or sometimes extended periods. Though there is much talk of whether someone is a slave at heart or a born Master, I think those discussions are better left to experienced members of the community. For a newcomer it is much easier to understand what we do if it is seen as "role play". Now that said, just because it can be described as "role play" doesn't mean it is not an integral part of who we are.

Let me emphasize that when I discuss terms like Daddy and boy in the BDSM sense, I am not talking about a boy as someone who is under the age of consent. The role of "boy" is not about age, but about having those characteristics of boyishness, a playful spirit with rebellious streak. The same holds true for the term "girl" when used in reference to people in our community. I just have to make that point emphatically to avoid any misunderstanding of our activities.

Since much of what I discuss is about the SM part of the acronym, I will concentrate on that for a moment. Sadomasochism, as practiced in the leather/BDSM community is not the pathological kind and probably has at times been more accurately called Sexual Magic. What we do in the dungeon and bedroom is all about sensations and the effects they have on our partners and ourselves. I like to think of our people as "differently pleasured". We find arousal and ultimately enjoyment in giving or receiving intense sensations and pain. I sometimes just lump everything in the category of kink, for the sake of brevity.

If you have a problem understanding that concept I will use an example that my friend Viola Johnson, a respected leatherwoman and author, uses when she addresses college classes. She asks them if anyone in the room is kinky. That question is usually met with snickers and no hands being raised. Then she asks if anyone has ever tasted a jalapeño pepper. Naturally many hands go up. She makes the point that jalapeños are hot and they burn your tongue. All heads usually nod in agreement. Then she says to lower your hands if you never ate a jalapeño again after the first taste. Almost no hands go down. She concludes with the pronouncement that "by definition, you are kinky!"

Her point is usually understood immediately. Something that is painful at first glance can actually be quite enjoyable. Just as jalapeños add spice to a meal, kink can add spice to a person's erotic enjoyment.

To stretch that analogy a little further, that spiciness is often an acquired taste. For some people it comes naturally and for others it never happens at all. That is as it should be, not everyone will enjoy everything. People in the SM community rarely participate in every conceivable SM activity. Some only dabble in the mild practices while other dive in head first and revel in the more extreme forms. Their intensity is not a measure of whether or not they are kinky; it's just a matter of how kinky they are.

If you spend any time in the BDSM community you will undoubtedly hear the phrase "safe, sane and consensual". This phrase was first used as a quick and easy shorthand to explain to people outside the community what we do. I understand it was first used by David Stein of GMSMA (Gay Men's SM Activists) to make a differentiation between the kind of play he liked and the criminally abusive acts often called SM by the press and law enforcement.

For my purposes I would define the terms as follows:

Safe - an act that consciously avoids any risks to health

Sane - participating only in a healthy state of mind, not under the influence of mind altering substances

Consensual - playing only with the full informed consent of everyone involved, and that all participants are of legal age of consent.

There are other definitions and this topic is one that causes endless discussions in the community, but the basics are pretty much the same. The reality is that for things to be safe, sane and consensual everyone has to be aware of any potential risks and willing to take responsibility for any consequences. It's all about being responsible.

Additionally all consensual BDSM scenes are negotiated. The negotiation may take the form of a detailed discussion of what will happen during a scene, or it can be a general agreement of the direction things will flow. Either way, there is usually a prearranged "safe word" or some other signal that either partner can use to bring the activity to a halt should they feel in danger or become too uncomfortable. There are very many ways to negotiate scenes and safe words, but I will not go into the details here.

Now, beyond the nuts and bolts of BDSM, of which there are numerous books on the subject, I would like to talk a little about the "why".

First and foremost for me and my partners is, it's enjoyable. That means that taken as a whole the positives of a scene outweigh the negatives. The experience is both satisfying and exciting and everyone involved goes home without permanent injuries or emotional pain. That doesn't mean that sometimes people don't end up with a few bruises or whelps from a well placed whip or paddle, but it does mean that they don't have any life threatening or body deforming after effects.

Now before you run away screaming, take this into consideration. Have you ever had a night of rough sex? By rough, I mean a sexual experience that was really intense and may have lasted a long time. I know I have and most everyone I know has as well. I am talking about the kind of sexual fun that might even leave you sore in the morning.

Now, if this describes something you did and you enjoyed it, consider what went through your mind every time you felt that soreness the next day. If you are like me, you recalled the previous evenings romp, got a little tingle and smiled. Well that is the same tingle someone who goes home with bruises from a night of SM feels the next day.

Now back to that night of rough sex. Perhaps your partner or you gave each other a few playful swats on the butt during the course of the evening. It was playful and sexy fun, and guess what? It was kinky! Erotic spanking is SM. I know lots of people who enjoy a little spanking during sex and they still have trouble understanding why I like playing with pain. Go figure!

Now consider bondage. In most cases bondage involves putting a person in some sort of restraining arrangement that limits their movement.

It can go so far as to limit their vision with a blindfold, their hearing with ear plugs and even their sense of touch by encasing most of the body in some sort of covering. Why would anyone enjoy this? Some bondage enthusiasts find the forced immobility somewhat freeing. By being restrained they can let go of the stress and strain of the day and just exist in the moment. It is a kind of enforced Zen for them.

For other people, bondage gives them permission to do something they would not normally give themselves permission to do. For example, a man who would never give himself permission to engage in oral sex with another man might absolutely love it if he was tied in a kneeling position and "forced" to do it. I put forced in quotation marks to indicate the fact that it would have been negotiated prior to the scene, and therefore it would actually be consensual. The trick in the mind of the person in bondage is that he or she had no choice once they were tied up. The reality is that they could have requested to be released with a prearranged "safe word" at any time. The mind is an interesting thing isn't it?

In extreme forms of bondage, people report having out-of-body experiences from the sensory deprivation. These take on an almost spiritual feeling for some people, and they can be very pleasurable for the person being bound.

I also used the word fetish in some of my descriptions. That one is easy to describe and understand. In regards to sexuality, a fetish is finding erotic qualities in inanimate objects. For example I like wearing leather when I play in the bedroom or dungeon. It enhances the sexual energy of the scene for me and as such it is a fetish. I like the feel and smell and look of leather, especially black leather. Boots, chaps, vests, shirts, pants, you name it.

Some men really love women's shoes. To them a woman wearing very spiked high heels is about as sexy an image as they can think of. It's a common fetish and one that has gained mainstream clout. The high heel has long been in fashion both on the street and in the bedroom.

Rubber is another popular fetish. Wearing rubber garments has a unique feel and look. Like leather, rubber can play a central part of a sexual encounter or just be an enhancement.

Fetishism in general has become more accepted than BDSM in the mainstream of society. A lot of this I would credit to performers like Madonna who wear fetish clothing in their stage performances and videos, but it dates back far beyond the modern times. Fetish wear appears in the earliest civilizations and will probably be around forever.

For most BDSM enthusiasts, their play incorporates many aspects of these different kinks. It is not uncommon for my scenes to involve leather, my personal fetish, as well as SM play and sometimes bondage as well. I like to consider it a sort of sensual smorgasbord at my disposal to create and enjoy with my play partners.

When I say play partners I am referring to people who I play with in the dungeon. They are not my sexual partners in the strictest sense. My boy and life partner fulfills that role just fine! However, we have an agreement that either of us can participate in BDSM scenes at play parties or private parties.

This is just a very brief overview of the BDSM/leather/fetish world. For additional information on BDSM, leather, and fetish topics I have provided a bibliography specifically devoted to that subject in a later appendix.

Appendix II

Kink in the Christian Closet

The kinds of things we do in our SM play are not new. People have been participating in these activities for ages. Beyond the erotic practice of SM, early Christians as well as other religions practiced what would today be seen as kink. These Christian ascetics often abstained from sexual relations and social contact as a means to find a deeper spiritual path, as well as penance and means to salvation. John the Baptist, many of the apostles and even Paul saw ascetic disciplines as means to enlightenment.

Later in Christian history sects such as the Cathars practiced ascetic rituals as means of purification. The word Catharsis comes from this early sect which was eventually driven out of the Christian Church. I suspect they were seen as too strange and politically incorrect. Sound familiar? Similar sects existed in Judaism of the time. The Essenes, the people who wrote and preserved what we now call the Dead Sea Scrolls lead a monastic existence and practiced abstinence as a means of preparing for a coming holy war. I have even read a few papers which connect Jesus to this sect.

More recent kinky ties are evident in the early 13th and 14th centuries when flagellation, what we now call flogging, was used by devout Christians as penance for their sins. The Catholic Church later condemned these adherents as heretics. A connection was seen between their actions and early Greek Dionysian practices and the church wanted a clean break with earlier religions.

What flagellants did was use whips and floggers on themselves and each other in grand ritual processions accompanied by prayer, chants and reading of the Psalms. I believe the expression "whipped into a frenzy" referred to the state of the participants in these rituals. Anyone who is in the SM scene knows the physical ecstatic state that can accompany a good flogging. Apparently, so did these early practitioners, but they interpreted the experience in a slightly different way.

The flagellant movement spread across Europe about the same time as the Black Death. Not surprisingly many of the flagellants believed their actions could atone for the punishment of the plague. The reality was that often time the flagellants actually brought the plague to towns and villages where it had yet to strike. Eventually many of these groups were denied entry into towns and villages and the practice faded. Additionally, the Inquisition found many ascetic Christians as heretics and they were killed and tortured to prevent their practices from spreading.

I suspect the popularity of flagellation which some historians refer to as a "mania" that attracted thousands of adherents was really the result of fear of the plague and other natural problems. Additionally, once a person participated in the practice, they became addicted to the activity. In an age where so much was prohibited by church doctrine, the cathartic release of the flogging must have been like a drug.

If you have ever experienced the "high" that comes after a good flogging or whip scene, then you can easily imagine why the practice became popular. It is also such a profound experience that it is also easy to imagine why it was seen as suspicious and potentially heretical by the church. Much of the history of the Christian church has focused on consolidating power and limiting the spiritual experiences of its followers to those sanctioned by clergy. People having cathartic experiences that could not be controlled by the church just wouldn't do.

Today, there are still a few groups of Christians who practice flagellation and even more severe forms of asceticism. In the Philippines, Christians often whip themselves as part of the preparation for Easter. Devout adherents even have themselves crucified as a sign of their devotion, though thankfully, they do not remain on the cross until death.

In Spain and Italy, once every seven years groups of Christians organize parades of flagellants in preparation for Lent. They whip themselves with linen floggers knotted at the ends to inflict severe pain. Often a priest walks behind them pricking their backs with sharp bits of glass producing a bloody spectacle. Others actually have glass in the knots of the floggers. Either way the participants move into the same state as someone in the dungeon or playroom. They alter their consciousness through physical means. In the dungeon we call it play and a fetish; in the processions they call it devotion. In reality I suspect it is a bit of both.

An interesting aspect of these kinds of events is the safety and practicality that is inherent in the practice. Making the floggers of fresh linen means that they will most likely be relatively clean; infection can be kept to a minimum. Using linen also absorbs blood that sometimes flows from participants backs. That minimizes the splattering of blood and possible contamination of bystanders, though some is surely flung from the ends of the floggers once they become saturated. Using a piece of broken glass to prick the backs of the flagellants minimizes the problems from using metal. Tetanus would be an obvious problem with many metals. No I am not saying these events are safe, sane and consensual, in the same way as BDSM play, but it is obvious there was some thought that went into it.

I have witnessed similar ascetic practices in Mexico. When I was a teenager, my family made trips to Mexico to visit friends and for vacations. I distinctly remember an afternoon near the Cathedral in Puebla where I saw several people walking on their knees toward the church steps. I asked our host, a well known doctor in the city, what they were doing and he explained that they were practicing penance for their sins or were performing an act of devotion in hopes of securing God's blessing. Several of the women moving slowly toward the church were bleeding from the knees, yet they seemed unaware of the pain as the chanted the rosary and manipulated their beads. I have since found that the practice of flagellation still occurs in Mexico in some out of the way towns around Lent.

I do not actively incorporate my BDSM play into my worship; I keep it as part of my sexual life. That does not mean that I separate my sexuality from my religion completely. It also doesn't mean that I do not incorporate some asceticism into my Christianity as well. Like many Christians I make a conscious effort to observe the Lenten season with some form of sacrifice. I prefer the act of fasting. From sunrise to sunset I eat nothing. I do drink liquids, including coffee and soft drinks, so I guess I am not as devout as some. Still, I find the practice really works for me. Fasting is a physical sacrifice with a spiritual significance. Much like the flagellants, it uses a physical means to achieve a spiritual result.

The result is not a high, as with flogging, but it is a constant reminder of why I am doing it. Every time my stomach rumbles, I remind myself of Jesus long fast in the wilderness. I remember how a small sacrifice makes the season just that much more meaningful to me. I also find that when I break the fast at night, I am more aware of the blessings I have in my life. A meal whenever I want is something much of the world cannot enjoy. When I say a blessing before eating during Lent, I can really express my gratitude at the grace God has shown me in my life. I also reflect on just how lucky I am to have been born into a family living in a country with such wealth. I remember that our place in the world is not some kind of cosmic reward for doing good. We are where we are, and it is our job to make the most of it. That doesn't mean stepping on others less fortunate than ourselves to climb higher on the economic ladder. It means working to bring betterment, justice and peace to as many people as we can.

Appendix III
Further Reading

I like to read and more often than not I am usually reading a book that is non-fiction. More specifically, I have always been fascinated with books on spiritual or historic subjects as well as BDSM/Leather. In the list below are books in my personal library that I found rich in ideas and information on my faith journey and in my leather life. I sincerely hope they may enrich the lives of other readers as they have mine.

Leather/BDSM/Fetish Books

Bean, Joseph. _Leathersex - A Guide for the Curious Outsider and the Serious Player_ .Los Angeles, CA: Daedalus Publishing 1994

Bean, Joseph. _Flogging_. San Francisco, CA: Greenery Press 2002

Bannon, Race. _Learning the Ropes_. Los Angeles, CA: Daedalus Publishing 1992

Baldwin, Guy, M.S. _Ties That Bind._ Los Angeles, CA: Daedalus Publishing 1993

Mains, Geoff. _Urban Aboriginal, A Celebration of Leathersexuality._ San

Francisco, CA: Gay sunshine Press 1984

Ricardo, Jack (Editor) . _Leathermen Speak Out_. Los Angeles, CA: Leyland Publications 1993

Thompson, Mark (Editor). _Leatherfolk._ Los Angeles, CA: Alyson Publications 1991

Townsend, Larry. _Leatherman's Handbook_. San Francisco, CA: Le Salon 1977. (Reprinted numerous times by various publishers)

Wiseman, Jay. _SM 101, A Realistic Introduction_. San Francisco, CA: Greenery Press 1992

Faith, Spirituality, Christianity

Crossan, John Dominic. _God and Empire: Jesus Against Rome, Then and Now_. San Francisco, CA: Harper San Francisco 2007

Gandhi (Robert Ellsberg, Editor). _Gandhi on Christianity_. Maryknoll, NY: Orbis Books 1991

Josephus, Flavius. _Jewish Antiquities_. Cambridge, MA: Harvard University Press 1965

Josephus, Flavius. _The Jewish War._ New York, NY: Penguin Classics 1981

King, Martin Luther, (James Melvin Washington - Editor). _A Testament of Hope: The Essential Writings and Speeches of Martin Luther_. San Francisco, CA: Harper Collins 1991

Lerner, Michael. _The Left Hand of God, Taking Back our Country from the Religious Right_. San Francisco, CA: Harper San Francisco 2006

Olan, Levi A. *Prophetic Faith and the Secular Age*. New York, NY: Institute of Jewish Studies 1982

Nicolson, Adam. *God's Secretaries: The Making of the King James Bible.* San Francisco, CA: Harper Collins 2003

Miller, Robert J. (Editor). *The Complete Gospels, Annotated Scholars Versio.,* San Francisco, CA: Harper Collins 1994

Piazza, Michael. *Holy Homosexuals: The Truth about Being Gay or Lesbian and Christian*. Dallas, TX: Sources of Hope 1995

Piazza, Michael. *Rainbow Family Values*. Dallas, TX: Sources of Hope 1995

Spong, John Shelby. *Rescuing the Bible from Fundamentalism*. San Francisco, CA: Harper San Francisco 1992

Spong, John Shelby. *Sins of Scripture*. San Francisco, CA: Harper Collins 2005

Spong, John Shelby. *Why Christianity Must Change or Die,* San Francisco, CA: Harper Collins 1998

Stone, Ken (Editor) *Queer Commentary and the Hebrew Bible*. Continuum International Publishing Group 2001

West, Mona (with Robert E. Goss). *Take Back the Word, A Queer Reading of the Bible*. Cleveland, OH: Pilgrim Press 2000

White, Mel. *Stranger at the Gate: To Be Gay and Christian in America.* New York, NY: Simon & Schuster 1994

White, Mel. *Religion Gone Bad: The Hidden Dangers of the Christian Right*. New York, NY: J.P. Tarcher/Penguin 2006

Wilson, Nancy. *Our Tribe: Queer Folks, God, Jesus, and the Bible*. San Francisco, CA: Harper San Francisco 1995

Bibles

King James Version (KJV) Bible. Plano, TX: Thomas Nelson Inc. 1981

New Revised Standard Version (NRSV) Bible. Grand Rapids, MI: Zondervan Publishing 2005

New International Version (NIV) Bible. Grand Rapids, MI: Zondervan Publishing 2001

The Holy Scriptures According to the Masoretic Text (Hebrew Testament). New York, NY: Jewish Publication Society of America 1917 (Newer versions are available)

Appendix IV

Resources and Contacts

For those who wish to get more information about the leather/BDSM/fetish scene or about my church and its parent denomination I include the following list of addresses and web sites.

National Leather Association – International   www.nla-i.com

National Coalition for Sexual Freedom   www.ncsfreedom.org

Cathedral of Hope (Dallas, TX)   www.cathedralofhope.com

United Church of Christ (National Headquarters)   www.ucc.org

Hope for Peace & Justice (Affiliated with COH)   www.h4pj.org

Whosoever.org (Gay Christian Site)   www.whosoever.org

About the Author
Hardy Haberman

Since the mid-70's Hardy has been active in the leather community and a member of many BDSM/Fetish organizations including Dallas Motorcycle Club, Leather Rose Society, NLA-Dallas, Discipline Corps and a founding member of Inquisition-Dallas. Considering himself a "Pain Technologist" he specializes in CBT and has an unusual fondness for clips clamps and clothespins, as well as more esoteric SM play.

Professionally he is a filmmaker. His documentary on the leather lifestyle "LEATHER" has won numerous awards and appeared in festivals around the world, and his latest film, "Out of the Darkness, The Reality of SM" is currently being used by health care professionals around the world. His non-leather projects include the documentary "The Big Fair" a look inside the State Fair of Texas, which is soon to be distributed.

Outside his filmmaking, he is a gay political activist, author & speaker on aspects of the SM/Leather scene. His first book "The Family Jewels, A guide to male genital play and torment" is available at bookstores everywhere.

He was awarded NLAI's *Man of the Year* award in 1999 and in 2007 he was honored with a *Lifetime Achievement Award* from the National Leather Association International. Since April, 1995, he and his boy Patrick have been living together in Dallas with their Feline Mistresses, Elvira and Samantha and newcomer Jack-The-Cat.

Hardy Haberman is also the Author of:

The Family Jewels: A Guide to Male Genital Play and Torment. (2001, Greenery Press)

More Family Jewels, Further Explorations in Male Genitorture. (2007, Nazca Plains Publishing)

Playing with Pain: Stories from My Life in Leather. (2007, Nazca Plains Publishing)

All books available at Amazon.com or your local bookstore.

www.ingramcontent.com/pod-product-compliance
Lightning Source LLC
Chambersburg PA
CBHW071229290326
41931CB00037B/2456

9 781934 625385